American History for Teens

An Enthralling Guide to Major Events and Figures in the History of the United States of America

© Copyright 2025 - All rights reserved.

The content contained within this book may not be reproduced, duplicated, or transmitted without direct written permission from the author or the publisher.

Under no circumstances will any blame or legal responsibility be held against the publisher, or author, for any damages, reparation, or monetary loss due to the information contained within this book, either directly or indirectly.

Legal Notice:

This book is copyright protected. It is only for personal use. You cannot amend, distribute, sell, use, quote, or paraphrase any part, or the content within this book, without the consent of the author or publisher.

Disclaimer Notice:

Please note the information contained within this document is for educational and entertainment purposes only. All effort has been executed to present accurate, up-to-date, reliable, and complete information. No warranties of any kind are declared or implied. Readers acknowledge that the author is not engaging in the rendering of legal, financial, medical, or professional advice. The content within this book has been derived from various sources. Please consult a licensed professional before attempting any techniques outlined in this book.

By reading this document, the reader agrees that under no circumstances is the author responsible for any losses, direct or indirect, that are incurred as a result of the use of the information contained within this document, including, but not limited to, errors, omissions, or inaccuracies.

Free limited time bonus

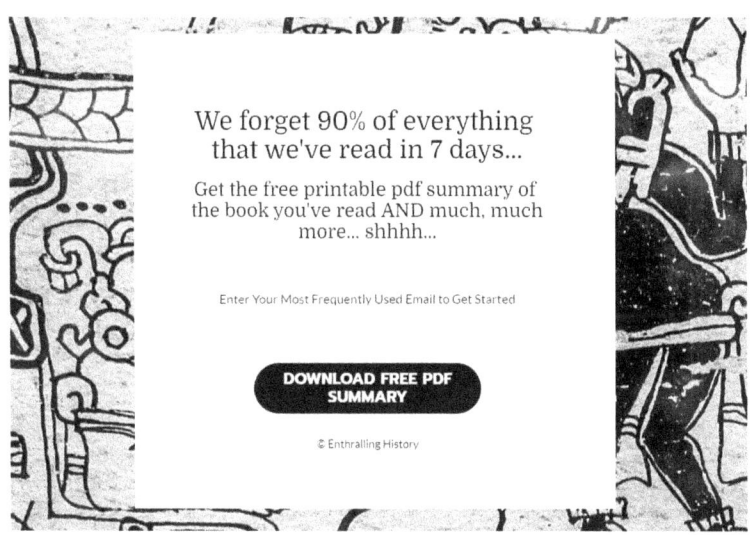

Stop for a moment. We have a free bonus set up for you. The problem is this: we forget 90% of everything that we read after 7 days. Crazy fact, right? Here's the solution: we've created a printable, 1-page pdf summary for this book that you're reading now. All you have to do to get your free pdf summary is to go to the following website: https://livetolearn.lpages.co/enthrallinghistory/

Or, Scan the QR code!

Once you do, it will be intuitive. Enjoy, and thank you!

Table of Contents

INTRODUCTION 1
CHAPTER 1: FOUNDATIONS 3
CHAPTER 2: THE COLONIAL PERIOD (1605-1760) 15
CHAPTER 3: REVOLUTION 27
CHAPTER 4: CIVIL WAR 40
CHAPTER 5: CIVIL RIGHTS 52
CHAPTER 6: THE WAR AGAINST THE WORLD 64
CHAPTER 7: THE SPACE RACE AND THE CUBAN ISSUE 78
CHAPTER 8: THE WAR ON TERROR 88
CHAPTER 9: PRESIDENTIAL PROGRESS 99
CHAPTER 10: STAR-SPANGLED HEROES AND VILLAINS 111
ANSWERS TO ROUNDUP QUESTIONS 122
HERE'S ANOTHER BOOK BY ENTHRALLING HISTORY THAT
YOU MIGHT LIKE 129
FREE LIMITED TIME BONUS 130
BIBLIOGRAPHY 131
IMAGE SOURCES 134

Introduction

America's history is like no other nation's. Its people came (and continue to come) from every corner of Earth. This diversity created an exciting blend of culture and new ways of doing things. Through hard work and fresh ideas, ordinary people still achieve the "American dream." The United States Constitution has protected people's rights and personal freedoms for over two hundred years.

Of course, it hasn't all been sunshine and rainbows. Many people came to America to escape oppression. They wanted a better life with bright opportunities. Yet, they displaced the people who were already in America. As the Native Americans curiously watched the colonists' ships appear on the horizon, did they have a clue that their way of life would soon end? Many ships arrived in colonial America with unwilling passengers. They had been ripped from their African homeland and shipped over as enslaved people.

Writing about America's history is complicated. There's so much information to pack in! What should be included? What, unfortunately, needs to be left out for lack of space? Should history focus only on famous people? What about all the ordinary people who made America what it is today?

This book will highlight the key events that shaped the United States of America and unwrap the stories of the resilient and brilliant people that made it happen. How did these people of the past think, feel, and act in their social and historical context? More than anything, America is a story of diverse people uniting to achieve exciting and exceptional goals. We'll explore the stories of "regular" people as well as the famous movers and shakers.

This history of America explains how we got where we are today. How did decisions made centuries ago impact how America's history unfolds? This is a key reason for diving into history. The past continues to influence the present. We'll investigate how some ideas were splendid successes. We'll also analyze the mistakes of the past that we want to avoid repeating.

America's history is an inspiring yet imperfect success story. Conflict and exploitation reared their ugly heads, and they still do. We cannot ignore or excuse the disturbing side of history, yet we can put it into perspective. America's founders were in uncharted territory. They were making it up as they went along while facing unimaginable challenges.

America's people have left an inspiring legacy. They had dreams and the tenacity, creativity, and competence to make them happen. America's founders set the course for the nation's government, economic system, and unique culture. Today, the United States of America is the most influential country on the planet. It has the world's largest economy and military and is the world leader in technology, innovation, and medical science. We have much to learn from America's mistakes and triumphs as its people overcame obstacles and forged an exceptional nation.

Chapter 1: Foundations

The first Americans were not the folks who stepped off the *Mayflower*. The Indigenous Americans had arrived thousands of years earlier. By the time the first European explorers and colonizers arrived from Spain and France, around ten million Indigenous Americans lived in what is now the United States.

How did the clash between the Indigenous Americans and colonizers play out? This chapter will unwrap the history of America's first people.

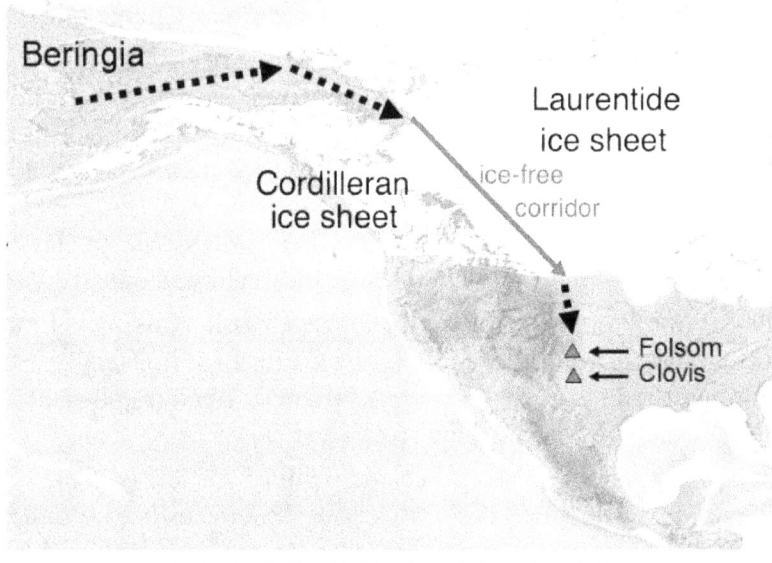

Beringia, the land bridge from Asia to America[1]

Who Were the Earliest Americans?

During the last ice age (the *Last Glacial Maximum*), people began migrating from Asia to North America. Dramatically lower sea levels uncovered a land area between Siberia and Alaska called **Beringia**. It was huge—twice as big as Texas! People and animals settled in Beringia. Some people crossed this land bridge into Alaska, following herds of woolly mammoths. As the ice age ended, the melting ice raised sea levels again. Beringia sank below the Bering Strait, so no one could walk into North America anymore.

The Clovis people were among the first tribes to enter North America and spread through the western United States. They were wandering nomads, following the mammoth, bison, and camel herds. Yes, America once had camels! These "camelops" had smaller humps and became extinct around eleven thousand years ago.

In Montana, construction workers accidentally uncovered the skulls and some bones of two little boys. One was two years old, and the other was around seven. According to radiocarbon testing, the Clovis people buried the toddler about twelve thousand years ago. His bones are the oldest human remains in the United States. Scientists named him Anzick after the family who owned the land. A nuclear genome study showed he came from Siberia, but baby Anzick's genes were closer to those of Indigenous Central and South Americans than North Americans. His tribe probably continued migrating south rather than settling down.

Later, another tribe passed through the area. They must have recognized it as a burial site. Baby Anzick was covered with red ochre, an iron oxide used in ancient burials worldwide. Tools and heirloom elk antlers surrounded him. The new tribe buried a seven-year-old boy twenty feet from Anzick. Because the burials were so close, archaeologists initially thought they were from the same era. However, radiocarbon dating puts them about three thousand years apart.

The earliest Americans spread throughout North America. Hundreds of tribes emerged with different languages, religions, housing styles, and government systems. At first, they hunted mammoths and giant armadillos called glyptodonts, the size of a small car.

The largest animals soon became extinct, probably from global warming and overhunting. The Indigenous Americans had to find other food sources. They fished, hunted smaller animals, and gathered berries and nuts. Eventually, they began farming. The Guilá Naquitz Cave in Mexico has evidence that Indigenous Americans were growing acorn squash by 6000 BCE. They soon began farming beans and maize (corn).

The Three Sisters planting system[2]

They grew these three crops in the "*Three Sisters*" planting system. The corn stalks were a trellis for the beans, and the beans fertilized the soil with nitrogen. The vines from the squash, grown between the corn stalks, shaded the ground, keeping it from drying out.

The Three Sisters planting system spread throughout North America. When the Europeans arrived, the Indigenous Americans taught them how to do it. The Native Americans also grew tobacco (for smoking in sacred ceremonies) and sunflowers (grinding the seeds into flour and making dye from the flowers).

Some of the Native Americans built cities. Cahokia (on the Mississippi River in Illinois) thrived in the 1100s CE. Its population of forty thousand people sprawled over six square miles, making it the largest city north of Mexico. It had 120 flat-topped mounds about 100 feet high with huge wooden temples at the top. Cahokia had a fifty-acre Grand Plaza for playing chunkey—a game in which a person threw a spear at a disk-shaped stone rolled over the ground.

A chunkey player³

Chaco Canyon in New Mexico housed thousands of people in tiered apartment buildings up to six stories high, built around 850 CE. These were the largest structures in North America for the next thousand years. One building, Pueblo Bonito, had 650 rooms. The Pueblo people built their apartments with three-foot thick walls using sandstone blocks and timber. Incredible networks of irrigation canals watered large farms outside the city.

The Indigenous Americans developed sophisticated political systems. Some used an early form of democracy, debating issues and making decisions as a group. However, they didn't emphasize individual freedoms as much as rule by the people as a whole.

The Huron (Wendat) Confederacy and Iroquois (Haudenosaunee) Confederacy formed alliances governed by clans. Membership in the clans passed from mother to child (and still does). Both men and women participated in government but in separate council meetings. The senior women advised on military and foreign policy issues. The councils decided things through negotiation and mutual agreement.

What Did the First European Explorers Discover?

The Norse Vikings were the first Europeans to sail to North America. Icelandic sagas said Leif Erikson led an expedition from Greenland to "Vinland" (Newfoundland). He had heard of the new land from other Vikings whose ship had been blown off course. They had sailed along the new land's coastline but headed back to Greenland without going to shore. Radiocarbon dating confirms Erikson briefly settled in Newfoundland around 1021 CE. Erikson wrote that they spent the winter there and returned to Greenland in the spring. Other Vikings continued to sail to Newfoundland for several decades but never established a permanent settlement.

Four centuries later, Christopher Columbus was born in Italy. He became a sailor at age fourteen and immediately fell in love with the sea. He soon became a highly skilled navigator. He believed that he could reach East Asia by crossing the Atlantic Ocean. He thought it would be quicker, safer, and easier than the complicated land and sea route people used in his day.

Columbus needed a sponsor to pay for his expedition, but Portugal and England turned him down. Finally, Queen Isabella and King Ferdinand of Spain gave him three ships. He set sail in 1492, crossing the Atlantic.

However, he thought the world was about a third smaller than it really is. Almost two thousand years earlier, the Greek mathematician Eratosthenes had calculated the circumference of the Earth and came amazingly close to today's calculations. Yet, Columbus misinterpreted the work of Eratosthenes and other early scholars.

After sailing for two months, Columbus reached an island of the Bahamas he named San Salvador. He planted a cross on its shore and led his crew in a prayer of thanksgiving. He sailed around several

Caribbean islands, thinking they were in the East Indies. One of his ships, the *Santa María*, wrecked off the coast of Hispaniola (today's Haiti and the Dominican Republic). He had to abandon the ship and left thirty-nine men behind to set up a colony.

Columbus lands in the New World.'

When Columbus returned to Spain, the king and queen made him governor of the new land. He sailed to the New World three more times. On his third voyage, he discovered South America, realizing it was a new continent. He spent his fourth voyage exploring Central America, trying to find a passage to Asia.

His attempts to govern the new land were unsuccessful. He was overly harsh to both the Indigenous people and the Spaniards he commanded. Nevertheless, his discovery of Central and South America opened the door to European colonization.

Who First Colonized the Land That Is Now the United States?

At first, the Norse Vikings of Greenland seemed interested in colonizing North America. However, they forgot about the new land as other problems distracted them. Their existence was threatened by lethal attacks by the Inuit people, climate change (it got a lot colder in an already cold country), and the plague. By 1540, the few Norse people who hadn't died abandoned Greenland.

Amazingly, it was almost two decades after Columbus died when the Spanish explorer Juan Ponce de León rediscovered North America. In 1513, Ponce de León waded ashore near today's St. Augustine, Floria, and planted the Spanish flag. Six years later, he brought fifty horses and two hundred people to establish a colony near today's Port Charlotte on Florida's southwest coast. However, fierce attacks by the Calusa people killed eighty of his men and wounded Ponce de León. The survivors retreated to Cuba.

In 1527, Pánfilo de Narváez led an expedition of six hundred men to explore Florida and set up colonies. Before even reaching Florida, a hurricane in the Caribbean sunk two of his ships. The remaining ships landed on Florida's west coast. Narváez sent three hundred men to hike up the coast, scouting out the area. Meanwhile, another one hundred men stayed on the ships sailing north. The two groups were supposed to meet at Tampa Bay, but that never happened. Narváez was confused about where he was. He thought Tampa Bay was north, but it was actually behind them, to the south.

The ships sailing up the coast looked for the land expedition but couldn't find it. Eventually, they gave up and sailed to Mexico. Led by Narváez, the land troops trudged north, dying from starvation, disease, and attacks by the Native Americans. They resorted to killing their horses and eating them. Finally, they made rafts and tried to sail to Mexico, but a storm killed all but eighty men, including Narváez. The survivors landed on Galveston Island off the Texas coast, where the Indigenous Americans enslaved them. Only four men managed to escape.

Álvar Núñez Cabeza de Vaca was one of the four escapees. It took him and his three companions eight years to make their way to the Spanish colonies in Mexico. On the way, they learned the Indigenous people's languages. The local people respected them as "children of the sun" who could pray over the sick, and they became well. These four men were the first Europeans known to explore what is now the southwestern United States.

In 1539, Spanish explorer Hernando de Soto launched an expedition to explore America's southeast. He landed at today's Tampa with three hundred horses and seven hundred men. His primary objective was finding gold, which did not pan out. His second goal was colonizing the area. He traveled north through today's Georgia, the Carolinas, and

Tennessee. He kept the Indigenous Americans at bay by sending his scouts to capture their chiefs and hold them hostage. He captured and enslaved other Native Americans, put collars around their necks attached to chains, and forced them to haul supplies and grind corn to feed his men.

Hernando de Soto[5]

However, de Soto's luck ran out when he passed through Alabama in 1540. This was the land of the powerful Coosa chiefdom, which ruled over a confederation of other tribes. De Soto's men captured Tuscaloosa, the Coosa chief. When de Soto demanded supplies, Tuscaloosa told him that the nearby town of Mabila had everything they needed. De Soto marched with Tuscaloosa to Mabila and entered the town immediately with his team, not waiting for the rest of his army.

A wall of wooden poles and woven vines slathered with clay surrounded Mabila. It had several watchtowers. Tuscaloosa distracted the Spaniards by having twenty teen girls perform a dance. Yet, they were the only women around. No children could be seen either. Most of the men were fixated on the dancing girls, but one soldier peeked into a house and saw armed men crouching inside. Meanwhile, Tuscaloosa slipped away.

Suddenly, the Coosa warriors poured out of the huts like maddened bees flying out of a hive. They sent a hail of arrows toward the Spaniards, panicking the horses and instantly killing several men. In the tight space, the Spaniards could not put their horses into play. They fled out of the town gates, which the Coosa barred behind them. At that point, the rest of de Soto's men arrived. The Spaniards hurled flaming torches over the walls of Mabila, setting the houses' thatched roofs on fire. Tuscaloosa died, along with around 2,500 of his men. Twenty-two conquistadors died, and hundreds suffered arrow wounds.

De Soto led his men west, discovering the Mississippi River. They built rafts, and as they crossed the river, two thousand Aquixo warriors paddled their canoes out to greet them. The Aquixo offered gifts to de Soto, communicating friendliness, but he ordered his men to fire on them.

That winter in Arkansas was bitterly cold. De Soto had lost half his horses and one-third of his men. He died of fever in 1542, never finding the gold he wanted nor establishing a permanent colony.

In 1559, Spanish explorer Tristán de Luna y Arellano tried again to colonize Florida, leading over fifteen hundred men to Pensacola Bay. He had been a conquistador in Mexico, conquering regions and setting up colonies there. But a hurricane struck before they even unloaded the ships, sinking most of his vessels and flooding the land. The survivors fled inland to Alabama and found an abandoned Indigenous village on the Alabama River. They stayed there through the winter, but a lack of food forced them to abandon the colony.

Meanwhile, France had become interested in Florida. In 1562, the French explorer Jean Ribault explored the peninsula. In 1564, the Protestant French Huguenot, René Goulaine de Laudonnière, built Fort Caroline on the St. Johns River, near today's Jacksonville.

Spain found this threatening since their ships followed the Gulf

Stream current along Florida's east coast before sailing across the Atlantic. Spanish colonizers in Mexico and Central America had finally found gold, and their ships carried treasures back to Spain.

The Spanish king, Philip II, assigned his best admiral, Don Pedro Menéndez de Avilés, to establish a colony on Florida's northeastern coast to defend against the French. In 1565, Avilés built St. Augustine with six hundred men, the first permanent colony in what would become the United States. His brilliant military maneuvers shut down the French Fort Caroline.

The Gonzalez-Alvarez House, built around 1723, the oldest surviving house in the continental United States' oldest city[6]

Once St. Augustine was established, Spain built other colonies in today's United States. In 1566, the Spanish built Santa Elena on Paris Island in South Carolina. In 1598, the Spaniards established a permanent colony in New Mexico, and in 1610, they built Santa Fe.

When Did the Slave Trade Begin?

The Indigenous Americans practiced slavery long before the European colonizers arrived. Their enslaved people were usually prisoners of war from other tribes. Slavery was especially rampant among the Aztec of Mexico, who needed a constant supply of sacrificial victims for their bloodthirsty gods. However, tribes like the Creek, Cherokee, and Iroquois used slaves for labor.

In 1415, the Portuguese began exploring West Africa's coast, looking for gold and other treasures. Although West Africa did have gold, the Portuguese developed another commodity: the sale of people. They began kidnapping Africans and selling them. In 1444, they sent 235 captured Africans to Portugal to sell as enslaved people. When the Portuguese started colonizing South America in 1500, they imported enslaved Africans to farm their plantations. For the next three centuries, more African slaves traveled to the Americas than European colonists.

Why didn't the Portuguese enslave the Indigenous Americans? They tried. For instance, de Soto used some of them as baggage carriers. However, the Indigenous people knew the land. It was too easy for them to escape and make their way back home. Furthermore, they had contacts with nearby tribes and could act as informants. The only way the colonizers could successfully use Indigenous Americans as slaves was to capture them in one place and then sell them in a faraway colony. For instance, they might transport them from Florida to Brazil.

Another issue was that the Native Americans had no immunity to diseases brought from Europe, like smallpox, measles, and typhus. These diseases wiped out the Indigenous Americans who came in close contact with the colonizers. At least 80 percent died in the first century after Columbus arrived. In 1537, Pope Paul III forbade the enslavement of Native Americans. Although it continued to an extent, the Spanish and Portuguese colonizers began importing enslaved Africans on a large scale.

Roundup Activity

Find the words in the puzzle. Then, write a definition of each word. Check your answers in the back of the book.

Word Search: America's Early Foundations

```
V K D P F T A C J V M U K Y O
A H V S P S H L C B Y M P U W
O N U F J T Y S A U D P Q Q C
K O Z R L Z H V H X R K Z A A
D X L I O P A P O V M C B E L
D P C E C N P R K Y Q O P R U
I C A F X K S A I P O L H A S
R O M G T U S C A L O O S A A
O L E W J Y P B R Z N N B M C
Q U L D B C G S M E M I X A O
U M O B E R I N G I A Z C I O
O B P O Y C R Z T F V E D Z S
I U S C L O V I S Y U R L E A
S S D K F A E K P V M S I Q L
C N K D R G S B J M T I W J O
```

Tuscaloosa   colonizers   Beringia
Iroquois   Anzick   camelops
Cahokia   Clovis   Hurons
Coosa   Columbus   Calusa
maize

Image source[7]

Chapter 2: The Colonial Period (1605-1760)

For several centuries, the British and others colonized the land that became the United States. This chapter dives into some key events and influences in this pivotal period. What challenges did the early colonists face? How did their values shape America? What transformed America's colonies?

How Did the Reformation Influence America's Colonization?

On October 31, 1517, a monk named Martin Luther nailed his *Ninety-five Theses* to Wittenberg Castle's door. He firmly stated that only the Bible had authority on matters of faith. Only faith in Jesus brought salvation. Martin Luther's ideas turned Europe upside-down. Thousands left the Roman Catholic Church to form new Protestant groups, like the Church of England, the Puritans, and the Baptists. Some of these groups had a fresh philosophy about government. For instance, many believed religion and government should be separate. The early Reformers suffered persecution in Europe for their beliefs. They were looking for a place to be free to practice what they believed were Biblical teachings on daily life, government, economics, and more.

The new colonies in America were remarkably progressive compared to the European countries they left. The colonists considered Europe's governments to be tyrannical. They felt that the abuses and corruption in the church made it a shadow of what it was meant to be. The colonies became a haven for groups escaping religious persecution. Of course, they didn't always do it perfectly, and disagreements on how things should be done led to messy situations.

The Jews also suffered under the Inquisition in Portugal and Spain. Muslims and Jews had to convert to Christianity or be burned at the stake. Thousands did convert, but then the rulers of Spain and Portugal suspected their conversions were fake. To escape this horrific treatment, about three thousand Jews immigrated to America in the colonial period. Many Muslims fled to North Africa, where they could legally practice Islam.

What Happened to the "Lost Colony?" (1585–90)

In 1585, Sir Walter Raleigh established America's first British colony on North Carolina's Outer Banks. After a failed first start, Sir Raleigh tried again. In 1587, 115 men, women, and children arrived on Roanoke Island. Their governor was John White. His pregnant daughter, Elizabeth Dare, gave birth in August 1987 to Virginia Dare, the first English child born in America. Shortly after, Governor White returned to England to organize more supplies.

A war between England and Spain delayed his return. When White returned to his colony three years later, no one was left on Roanoke Island. They found fresh tracks but no people. The word "Croatoan" was carved into a post. White assumed the colony had fled to nearby Croatoan Island after a hostile attack by the Indigenous people. However, expeditions to find the missing colonists turned up nothing.

The Lost Colony, painted by colonist John White[9]

Who Settled Jamestown, the First Permanent English Colony? (1607)

The Virginia Colony was America's first successful English colony. Three ships holding 149 men and boys arrived in today's Virginia in 1607. One of their council leaders was John Smith, who was once a pirate and a slave. How did that happen? He was shipwrecked off the coast of France and then rescued by pirates, whom he joined for a time. Later, he was captured in battle while helping Austria fight the Turks. The Turks took him to Constantinople (today's Istanbul) as an enslaved person, shaved his head, put an iron ring around his neck, and often beat him. He finally escaped, returned to England, and joined the colonists heading to Virginia.

The colonists settled their new town on the James River. They named it Jamestown after King James I (the same king who commissioned the King James Bible). Two weeks after the colonists landed, the Powhatan tribe attacked, killing two Englishmen and wounding several others. More trouble ensued. The colonists needed safe drinking water and ran out of food. By September, sixty men had died.

John Smith and several other men were scouting for food and water when they ran into hunters from the Powhatan tribe. The Powhatans killed everyone but Smith and took him as their prisoner. The chief planned to kill Smith, but his ten-year-old daughter, Pocahontas, suddenly wrapped her arms around Smith's head, laid her head on his, and begged her father to spare him.

Chief Powhatan let Smith return to Jamestown and even sent food for the hungry colonists. He negotiated peace between the English and the other Indigenous tribes in the region. More ships arrived with new settlers, including the first women, but not enough food to sustain the growing settlement. Few of the colonists had been farmers in England. Some came from the upper class and were unwilling to work in the fields.

Unfortunately, a gunpowder explosion injured Smith's eye. He sailed to England for treatment, never returning to Jamestown. After he left, the settlers' relationship with the Powhatan tribe deteriorated. They demanded food from the tribespeople as if they were owed it. They kidnapped Pocahontas, using her as a bargaining chip. The Rev. Alexander Whitaker taught her English and how to read. She became a Christian and married John Rolfe, a prosperous tobacco farmer. (The Powhatans had taught the settlers how to grow and use tobacco.)

Pocahontas in British clothing, based on an engraving by Simon de Passe[9]

A group of Africans arrived in Jamestown in 1619. They had been kidnapped by the Portuguese, branded, chained, and forced into the hold of a slave ship packed so tightly that they could not move. Their ship was bound for Mexico when pirates attacked and took the enslaved people. The pirates sailed to Jamestown and exchanged around thirty Africans for food and supplies.

Slavery was not legal in England. Yet, the Jamestown colonists desperately needed workers to farm the land and build infrastructure. They had been bringing indentured servants from England. These petty criminals and desperately poor people served for about seven years. They then became free and usually got a plot of land. The Jamestown colonists decided to make the Africans indentured servants. Two Africans, Isabella and Anthony, worked for William Tucker. They had a son named William in 1624. He was the first African child born and baptized in the English colonies of America.

What Brought the Puritans to America? (1620)

The Puritans were Christians who thought that the Church of England needed more reform. Although it had separated from the Roman Catholic Church, it still held many beliefs and practices that the Puritans thought were unbiblical. After enduring persecution in England, many Puritans headed to Holland, which had more religious freedom. They were free in Holland but felt the culture was *too* free. They worried that their children would be led astray.

The Puritans decided to immigrate to America to set up their own colony with their own values. In 1620, 102 pilgrims sailed on the *Mayflower* to America. One young man, John Howland, was on the deck when a large wave suddenly swept him overboard. He would have surely died except that a rope was trailing behind the ship. He managed to grab the rope and was pulled back to safety. He and his wife eventually had ten children, and their descendants included three presidents (Franklin Roosevelt and both Bushes) and the poets Henry Wadsworth Longfellow and Ralph Waldo Emerson.

The Puritans originally planned to settle in the northern part of the Virginia Colony. They got permission to do this, but a storm blew them off course. They finally weighed anchor much further north, off Cape Cod in Massachusetts. Since this region was outside British jurisdiction, they formed their own governmental system called **The Mayflower Compact**. Based on the agreement of the majority, the men wrote up a set of laws they would follow. They pledged their continued loyalty to King James I; however, they made it clear they intended to self-govern as a society of equals. Forty-one men, including two indentured servants, signed the compact.

The Plymouth Colony suffered in its early days. The pilgrims arrived in November when the cold and snow had already set in. Most were sick, and only a few were strong enough to forage for food and water. Half of the colonists died in that brutal winter. The *Mayflower* had moored for the winter at Cape Cod, yet, astoundingly, when it sailed back to England in the spring, no colonist chose to return. They were committed to sticking it out.

Samoset introduces himself to the Puritans.[10]

How Did the Indigenous People Help the Puritan Colonists?

In the spring, the Puritans met the Indigenous Americans for the first time. A man named Samoset walked into their village. To their astonishment, he spoke to them in broken English. He told them he had become friends with English fishermen who came to the area in the summer. He said the fierce Patuxet people had recently lived where the Puritans had settled, but a plague had wiped them out (probably something like smallpox brought by the Europeans). Samoset was from the Abenaki tribe in Maine but was staying with the local Wampanoag people. He told them he would introduce them to the tribe.

Several days later, Samoset arrived with Chief Massasoit and several men with whom the Puritans made a peace treaty. One of the men who visited was Squanto, a Patuxet with an incredible story. An English explorer had kidnapped Squanto and twenty-six other Patuxet. He took them to Spain and sold them as enslaved people, but some Catholic friars bought the Patuxet people and freed them. Squanto traveled to England, where he worked as a shipbuilder. Because he had learned Spanish, English, and several Native American languages, he became an interpreter on a trade ship to get passage back home.

When Squanto reached Massachusetts, he discovered the plague had wiped out his tribe. Like Samoset, he found a home with the Wampanoag people. Squanto joined the Puritans and was invaluable. He taught them how to fish, hunt, and farm like the Native Americans. He also taught them how to live peacefully with the neighboring Indigenous people. For instance, the Puritans habitually purchased the land for their colonies from the local tribes.

The Puritans starved in their first winter. However, as the second winter approached, they had adequate food stores thanks to their Indigenous friends, especially Squanto. Governor William Bradford announced a day of thanksgiving to celebrate a good harvest and their freedom to live and worship as they chose. They invited the Wampanoag to join them, and ninety came to the feast of turkey, deer, lobster, eel, cornbread, and pies. Their Wampanoag friends stayed three days, and everyone enjoyed races, wrestling contests, and shooting competitions.

The Puritans and Wampanoag enjoy a thanksgiving feast[11]

At this time, the colony had twenty-two men, four women, fourteen teens, and thirteen small children. In the late fall, thirty-five more colonists arrived, to everyone's happy surprise. Unfortunately, they had not brought any extra food or supplies, so the Puritans had to divide up what they had. With hard work and Squanto's help, the Puritans made it through the second winter.

How Did the Puritans Shape American Values?

A problem Jamestown experienced was that some of the colonists were unwilling to put in the challenging work of farming and building. The Puritans also experienced some lazy colonists at first. However, they applied this biblical teaching: "But if any provide not for his own, and specially for those of his own house, he hath denied the faith, and is worse than an infidel" (I Timothy 5:8, KJV). The value of hard work and self-reliance became core American values.

The Puritans also had a spirit of toughness in the face of adversity. Their problems engendered innovation, as the Puritans had to learn how to survive in a completely different world. Other Puritan values that influenced America were individual freedom, self-government, self-improvement, and building wealth through free enterprise. They believed that anyone could be successful if they applied themselves.

The Puritans were dedicated to quality education from primary school through college. They believed that boys and girls needed to be literate so they could read the Bible for themselves. They paid for schools through public money and required all children to attend. The literacy rate of Puritan colonies was much higher than that of the colonies to the south. The Puritans founded Harvard College in 1636 and Yale in 1701.

What Were Other Early Colonies?

The Puritans established colonies in Connecticut, Massachusetts, New Hampshire, and Rhode Island. British Catholics established Maryland as a tobacco-growing colony in 1634. The Dutch founded New Netherland in 1624, which became New York. Sweden settled Delaware in 1638, and the Swedes and Dutch settled New Jersey. In 1661, England took over all these colonies, and in 1663, they took the Carolinas. In 1681, a

Quaker named William Penn colonized Pennsylvania and absorbed Delaware, although it was still a separate state. The British colonized Georgia in 1733. These colonies, along with Virginia, were all under British control by the mid-1700s.

How Did St. Augustine Become the First "Underground Railroad?"

Although slavery never became legal in England, the British colonies in America got involved in slavery. In the early days, the colonies used indentured servants to help farm their plantations. Half of the immigrants from England to Virginia were indentured servants. To the south, Spain and Portugal were importing thousands of enslaved Africans for the plantations in Brazil, the Caribbean, and Mexico.

Jamestown was the first to use Africans as indentured servants. They were supposed to release them after they completed their indenture. However, in 1640, an African indentured servant named John Punch ran away from his plantation with two White indentured servants. They were all captured, and the White men got a year added to their indenture as punishment for running away. However, John Punch received lifelong slavery as his penalty for the same thing. Within a year, Massachusetts became the first colony to legalize slavery, and the other colonies quickly followed. By 1700, the British colonies had close to 16,000 enslaved people.

Meanwhile, the Spanish colonists in Florida had been importing enslaved people since establishing St. Augustine in 1565. However, the Spanish king granted freedom to any slaves who escaped the British colonies and came to Florida. All they had to do was become Catholic and serve in the military for four years. The idea was to cripple the British colonies by reducing their labor force while building up Florida's military. The Spaniards settled the freed slaves at Fort Mose, just north of St. Augustine. Ironically, the Spaniards in Florida did not free their own slaves.

What Was the Great Awakening? (1730s–70s)

The Great Awakening was an extraordinary surge in Christian faith and enthusiasm that left a lasting impact on Britain and America. Thousands became Christians, and thousands more renewed their Christian faith.

Benjamin Franklin wrote, "One could not walk through the town in an evening without hearing Psalms sung in different families of every street."

Jonathan Edwards was a Congregationalist pastor invited to speak in Enfield, Connecticut, a congregation with little interest in spiritual things. Edwards dusted off a sermon he'd already preached in his church in Northampton. He was not an electrifying, Bible-thumping preacher. He read his sermon, *Sinners in the Hands of an Angry God,* in a monotone without looking out at the congregation.

Jonathan Edwards, engraved by R. Babson & J. Andrews [19]

Yet, as Edwards preached, the atmosphere in the church changed. People began shrieking and weeping as they recognized their sin. Edwards paused, waiting for people to regain their composure. As they quieted, he assured them that Jesus had "flung the door of mercy wide open and [stood] in the door crying and calling with a loud voice to poor sinners."

Another great preacher of the Great Awakening was the British minister George Whitfield. He was a friend of John and Charles Wesley, who were stirring up revival in England. Whitfield traveled through America's colonies, preaching to large outdoor crowds.

Some Christians began to question infant baptism, saying it wasn't anywhere in the Bible. These "Separatists" broke off to form new churches, especially Baptists and Methodists. It was the birth of evangelical Christianity.

The Great Awakening doubled church membership in New England. Edwards, Whitfield, and other preachers emphasized a personal conversion experience and intimacy with the Holy Spirit. As people gathered in churches and homes, emotionally singing and praying, some spoke in unknown tongues and experienced physical healing.

Roundup Activity: Fill in the Blank

Place the correct words and phrases from the list below in the chapter summary. Check your answers in the back of the book.

Carolina	Fort Mose	George Whitfield	Holland	literate
John Smith	Jonathan Edwards	Protestant	Squanto	

Most of the colonists in Virginia and New England came from _____ groups. The Lost Colony disappeared from _____'s Outer Banks. Among Jamestown's early leaders, _____ _____ was a former pirate and slave. After leaving England, the Puritans first went to _____ before sailing to America. _____, a Patuxet man, taught the Puritans to farm, hunt, and fish. The Puritans believed all children needed to be _____. The Spaniards in Florida offered freedom to slaves who escaped the British colonies and settled them at _____ _____. _____ and _____ were two ministers who helped spark the Great Awakening.

Chapter 3: Revolution

Twelve years before the American Revolution, the British won an astounding victory in the French and Indian War, quadrupling the size of its American colonies. Patriotism was at an all-time high among the colonists. How did it all come crashing down? What were the seeds of the revolution? Why was the American Revolutionary War arguably among the most critical events in world history? Let's explore!

How Did the French and Indian War Change the Colonies? (1754–63)

In 1754, conflict erupted between America's British, Spanish, and French colonies. It started in Pennsylvania when the French and British both claimed an area in the Allegheny Mountains. George Washington, twenty-two at the time, outwitted a French ambush with his Seneca allies. However, while Washington was negotiating peace terms with the French commander, the Seneca chief suddenly planted his hatchet in the Frenchman's head. Negotiations fell apart, and the war began.

At this point, Britain controlled the colonies stretching from New Hampshire to Georgia. The French territory reached from Canada through the Midwest and down to Alabama, Mississippi, and Louisiana. Spain controlled Florida and the Southwest. France and Britain argued over who owned the Ohio River Valley of southwestern New York, western Pennsylvania, Ohio, West Virginia, Indiana, Kentucky, and Tennessee.

Some Indigenous American tribes allied with the French, and some with the British. The Iroquois Nation and Cherokees supported the British. This war was part of a global conflict—the *Seven Years' War*—that pitted Great Britain and Prussia against France, Spain, Russia, Sweden, and Saxony. The 1763 *Treaty of Paris* ended both wars. The British added everything east of the Mississippi to its territories. Britain also gave Cuba to Spain in exchange for Florida. Spain got most of France's territory west of the Mississippi.

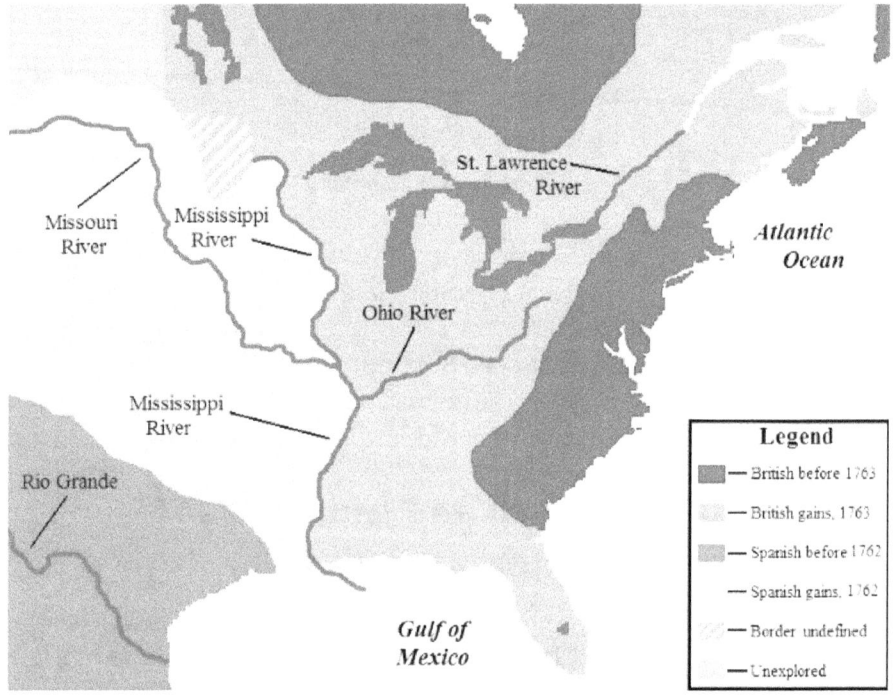

Territory at the end of the French and Indian War [18]

How Did the "Enlightenment" Influence the Colonies?

The Enlightenment was an intellectual trend in the seventeenth and eighteenth centuries that placed reason over faith and tradition. In Europe, many Enlightenment thinkers were also agnostic or atheist, believing one could not be both an intellectual and a Christian. However, many American Enlightenment thinkers still believed in God. Nevertheless, they thought philosophy and science were the answers to their problems.

A key American Enlightenment figure was Benjamin Franklin. He came from a profoundly religious Puritan family. Yet, as a teen, he embraced deism, which says that God created the world but then left it to run itself. Franklin believed religion was valuable because it taught moral behavior, which an orderly society needed. That's why he approved of the Great Awakening, although some folks said it was "anti-intellectual." Both the Enlightenment and the Great Awakening led to a change in thinking. People began to question tradition and governmental authority.

How Did Mercantilism and Other Issues Create Unrest?

Britain (and other countries) had colonies to increase their wealth and access to resources. Britain controlled the price of cotton, tobacco, and gold from the colonies. England's trade regulations discouraged their colonies from trading with other countries.

England also discouraged industries in the colonies. They wanted them to send raw goods, like timber, cotton, and precious metals, to England. The colonists then had to buy things from England made from raw goods. This is called ***mercantilism***—the attempt to build power and prosperity through one-sided trade. This approach led to tension between the colonies and England as the colonists felt Britain was exploiting them.

Britain began to demand more from the colonies after the Seven Years' War, which had emptied Britain's treasury and sunk it deep into debt. Britain's young King George III felt it was fair for the colonists to pay taxes on things like coffee, sugar, and wine to help pay the debt. In 1765, Parliament introduced the ***Stamp Act***, a tax on documents in the colonies. Almost all documents, even the newspapers, were printed on stamped paper, so they had to be taxed.

Benjamin Franklin thought the taxes were reasonable. However, many colonists grumbled, "We have no American seats in the Parliament. How can we be taxed when no one speaks for us?"

The British leaders replied, "You are *virtually* represented! You are right—you can't vote for members of Parliament, but neither can women or poor people here. Nevertheless, we're looking out for their best interests, just like we're looking out for yours."

Benjamin Franklin by Joseph-Siffred Duplessis, circa 1778[14]

A young lawyer named Patrick Henry published a list of reasons why the Stamp Act was illegal. Britain began having second thoughts. They called Benjamin Franklin over to testify before Parliament. Although Franklin didn't personally object to the Stamp Act, he was brutally honest with Parliament on its impact on American morale.

"What was the temper of America toward Great Britain before the year 1763?"

"The best in the world!" Franklin answered. "They submitted willingly to the government of the Crown."

"And what is their temper now?"

"O, very much altered."

The Parliament asked Franklin if the colonists would submit to the Stamp Act if they removed the obnoxious parts. He shook his head. "No, they will never submit to it."[i]

---

[i] Thomas Kidd, *American History, Combined Edition: 1492-Present* (B&H Academic, 2019).

What Led up to the Boston Tea Party?

Parliament repealed the Stamp Act in 1766, but they passed the *Townshend Acts* the following year—more taxes and regulations. The first act punished New York for not supporting the British soldiers in their colony. The second act taxed glass, lead, paint, paper, and tea shipped from Britain to America. The third act was a system to collect taxes, and the fourth act removed shipping fees for the British sending tea to America.

The indignant colonists sputtered, "Well, in that case, we won't import goods from Britain!"

In 1768, four thousand British soldiers were stationed in Boston.

"Why did they send so many soldiers?" people anxiously wondered. "We have only 16,000 people in Boston, including women and children!"

In 1770, an unruly crowd gathered in Boston, heckling the British soldiers and throwing snowballs at them. The British shot into the crowd, killing five colonists and wounding six others. After this, the British repealed most of the Townshend Acts. Yet, they kept the tax on tea. "We still have sovereign authority to tax the colonies!"

In response, the American colonists stopped buying tea. They began growing their own herbal teas or drinking coffee. Drinking regular tea became "un-American."

Losing the American market devastated the British-owned East India Company. The British tried to fix the problem with a new bill in 1773 that reduced the tea tax. However, it only allowed a few colonists loyal to the Crown to act as tea agents.

"Send it back!" the American patriots roared, blocking tea shipments into New York and Philadelphia.

In Boston, a group of patriots disguised themselves by rubbing soot on their faces and dressing as Native Americans. They boarded the tea ships, broke 342 crates open, and dumped the tea into Boston Harbor. The "Boston Tea Party" enraged the British Parliament. Britain closed Boston Harbor to all merchant ships. It also reworked Massachusetts' government, giving power to royal appointees.

The colonists were appalled. "Massachusetts had a legally elected government! How could the British shut it down? What will happen to our other colonies? We must get all the colonies together and discuss our next actions!"

What Did the First Continental Congress Decide? (1774)

Delegates from every colony except Georgia gathered in Philadelphia for the *First Continental Congress*. Leaders in the group included George Washington, Patrick Henry, and Samuel Adams. Adams was a radical who wanted to escalate the resistance movement. Others want to avoid goading Britain any further. Paul Revere brought the "Suffolk Resolves" from Massachusetts, demanding that the colonists resist any further actions of Britain to "enslave America."

"We must prepare a military for self-defense and end all commerce with Britain!"

The Continental Congress adopted a *Declaration of Rights*, which said the colonists were "entitled to life, liberty, and property."

"We should have the same rights and freedoms as the people living in England!"

The Congress also formed an association of seven thousand men to enforce a ban on British trade with America. Patriotic women formed groups to educate other women about substitutes for British goods. They shamed anyone they found out was using them. Conversations among patriotic women often sounded something like this:

"Ladies, did you hear that Mrs. Appleton is still drinking tea?"

A collective gasp rose from the women bending over their needlework.

One woman cleared her throat. "We must explain to her that coffee is patriotic. It's the American way!"

"Hear! Hear!" the other ladies murmured.

"Give Me Liberty or Give Me Death!"

In March 1775, Patriot Patrick Henry was a delegate to the Second Virginia Convention, which discussed an independent militia. Thomas Jefferson and George Washington attended. Patrick Henry defended the need for an American army: "The war is inevitable, and let it come! ... Is life so dear, or peace so sweet, as to be purchased at the price of chains and slavery? Forbid it, Almighty God! I know not what course others may take; but as for me, give me liberty or give me death!"[i]

"The Shot Heard Round the World"

No one technically declared war, but it began anyway. The British heard that the colonists had a cache of weapons in Concord, Massachusetts. On April 18, 1775, the British "Redcoats" marched on Concord by night. The "Sons of Liberty," a clandestine patriot group, had an alert system set up using lanterns and horseback riders. Paul Revere and William Dawes raced by horseback to Lexington, alerting their riders on the way.

Paul Revere's Ride[15]

---

[i] Thomas S. Kidd, *Patrick Henry: First Among Patriots* (Basic Books, 2011), 52.

The Massachusetts colonists quickly mobilized to fight the British in the Battles of Lexington and Concord. It began with "the shot heard round the world" in Lexington. No one was sure where the first shot came from. Was it a British or American soldier? Yet, once that shot rang out, the bullets flew. The British shot eight Americans and headed to Concord, where they faced a formidable defense. It was a swift victory for the colonists, who chased the Redcoats back to Boston. Ralph Waldo Emerson immortalized the first gunshot in his 1837 poem "Concord Hymn."

Three weeks later, the Green Mountain Boys, a Vermont militia, attacked Fort Ticonderoga on Lake Champlain. Their dawn attack surprised and quickly overcame the sleeping British. After the Green Mountain Boys' victory, they sent the fort's cannons to the American forces outside Boston to use in their siege against the city.

The Battle of Bunker (Breed's) Hill (June 1775)

On June 14, 1775, the Second Continental Congress authorized a Continental Army commanded by George Washington. On June 17, the British and the Americans clashed in the Battle of Bunker Hill outside Boston. Technically, the British won, as the Americans retreated. However, 1,054 British were killed or wounded compared to 450 Americans who were killed, captured, or injured. The inexperienced American militia proved they had what it took to fight the British army.

The Boston Siege (1776)

In the spring of 1776, George Washington's troops attacked Boston again. With the Americans surrounding Boston, the British could only get supplies or reinforcements by sea. However, Washington commissioned local fishing boats to interfere with these shipments. Over the winter, the Americans had dragged the canons from Ticonderoga on sleds over the snow to Boston's outskirts. They set their canons up at high spots around Boston and began bombarding the British on March 2. The British shot back, but their smaller cannons were out of range. On March 17, about ten thousand British troops fled Boston by ship.

The Declaration of Independence (July 4, 1776)

Heady with their early victories, the Continental Congress met in Philadelphia to formally declare that the thirteen colonies were independent. The Declaration of Independence stated: "We hold these truths to be self-evident, that all men are created equal, that they are endowed by their Creator with certain unalienable Rights, that among these are Life, Liberty and the pursuit of Happiness."

The declaration explained that when a government becomes destructive, it is the people's right to change or end it. It then listed King George's tyrannical acts against the Americans. The declaration dissolved America's political connection to Britain.

Crossing the Delaware by Emanuel Leutz[16]

Battle of Trenton (Christmas 1776)

The euphoria from the spring victory melted away in the fall when the Americans lost three battles in New York and New Jersey. The loss at Manhattan was especially disastrous. The Americans had quickly built Fort Washington overlooking the harbor, and General Nathanael Greene was busy sinking British ships. That's when British General William Howe decided to take out the American fort with his 8,000 British forces. General Washington was on the other side of the Hudson, unable to help the men in Manhattan. The Americans fought bravely but ultimately surrendered on November 16, 1776.

Washington and his demoralized men fled to Pennsylvania, where they camped by the Delaware River. Copies of Thomas Paine's booklet *Common Sense* circulated through the troops, giving them fresh encouragement: "The cause of America is in a great measure the cause of all mankind." Paine criticized the kingship system: "'Tis a form of government which the word of God bears testimony against, and blood will attend it." Paine laid out what an ideal government might look like, led by a president, with each colony represented by delegates. Paine challenged his readers, "A government of our own is a natural right."

With their resolve strengthened, Washington's men rowed over the Delaware on a dark and icy Christmas Eve. They marched to Trenton, arriving at dawn and surprising the Hessian soldiers (Germans hired by the British). Some of the Hessians escaped, but after their leader, Colonel Johann Rall, died from a gunshot, the rest surrendered. The Battle of Trenton brought a welcome victory on Christmas Day with captured food and supplies. With emboldened troops and restored morale, Washington scored another stunning triumph a week later at Princeton.

Battle of Saratoga (September–October 1777)

This pivotal battle took place just north of today's Albany, New York. Eight thousand British troops were marching south from Canada, led by General John Burgoyne. Thirteen thousand Americans, led by General Horatio Gates, wanted to block them from the Hudson River Valley. With greater numbers and assistance from French cannons, the Americans prevailed. The victory helped convince France to throw its support firmly behind the Americans.

The Battle of Yorktown Ends the War (September–October 1781)

The war had been dragging on for six years. Everyone was weary. The Americans were low on food and deep in war debt. Britain was simultaneously fighting France and Spain. General Washington had to decide: should he make another strike on New York City and wrap things up there, or should he march south and face off against General Cornwallis in Virginia? Washington gambled on Virginia.

His French ally, Lt. Gen. Comte de Rochambeau, promised the French forces would support the Americans. Washington had almost twenty thousand French and American troops, yet the British only had nine thousand in Virginia. Most of their army was in New York, where they expected Washington to attack. As Washington marched south, the French Navy blocked the British Royal Navy from entering Chesapeake Bay.

On September 28, the American army arrived at Yorktown and began digging trenches around the city. The British tried firing on the ditch diggers but were low on ammunition. The serious fighting began on October 9. Washington's canons pummeled the British for five days. Clouds covered the moon on October 14, and under cover of darkness, the Americans launched a surprise attack on the British fortifications outside the city.

On October 17, the Americans saw a drummer boy on a parapet, beating the rhythm to "Parley" (discussion of terms). Next to him stood a British officer waving a white handkerchief. The British had lost about 8,500 men compared to under 400 Americans and French. The British war machine had collapsed. When word reached Britain, Prime Minister North sighed, "Oh God. It is all over. It is all over."

The Peace of Paris (1783)

Several months later, Parliament authorized peace terms with America. It took two years of diplomatic negotiations to hash out the terms. The ***Peace of Paris***, signed on September 3, 1783, officially ended the war. It recognized the United States as an independent nation with the Mississippi River as its western boundary. Britain gave Florida back to Spain.

How Did the Constitution and the Bill of Rights Shape the New Nation?

Written in 1787 and put into action in 1789, the United States Constitution created America's government. It separated the government into three branches: legislative, executive, and judicial. The legislative branch (Congress) makes the laws. The executive branch carries out the laws. It includes the president and his or her Cabinet and federal agencies. The judicial branch (the Supreme Court and lesser courts) evaluates and interprets laws. On April 30, 1789, George Washington became the United States' first president.

George Washington by James Peale, circa 1782[17]

Within two years, the new American leaders realized they had forgotten to include fundamental human rights in the Constitution. So, they added the ***Bill of Rights*** as the first ten amendments to the Constitution. They provided for the protection of private property, protection from unreasonable searches and cruel punishment, and the right to free speech, carry arms, gather peacefully, practice one's religion, and have a speedy and fair trial.

Roundup Activity: True or False?

Mark each question "T" or "F." Check your answers in the back of the book.

( ) 1. The 1763 Treaty of Paris gave the French all the colonies east of the Mississippi River.

( ) 2. The Enlightenment thinkers preferred intellectual reason over faith and tradition.

( ) 3. The British trade policies with the American colonists were fair and profitable for all.

( ) 4. The Boston Tea Party led to the British closing Boston Harbor.

( ) 5. The Green Mountain Boys sent the canons from Fort Ticonderoga to Boston.

( ) 6. The Continental Congress wrote the Declaration of Independence at the war's end.

( ) 7. Thomas Paine's booklet *Common Sense* strengthened the resolve of the Americans.

( ) 8. Washington's troops won the Battle of Trenton on Christmas Day.

( ) 9. The Treaty of Paris recognized American independence and gave Florida back to Spain.

( ) 10. The Bill of Rights included freedom of speech and religion.

Chapter 4: Civil War

The Revolutionary War created the United States of America yet left unfinished business. The Declaration of Independence says all people are created equal. They have God-given rights to liberty and the pursuit of happiness. Was everyone in America truly equal in 1776? The half-million enslaved people were not. They did not have freedom and could not pursue happiness. In less than a century, the number of slaves morphed to four million!

The Civil War (1861–65) freed the enslaved people, which was the fundamental cause of the war. Yet the war also tackled another question: Could states just *secede* (drop out) if they were unhappy with the central government? Could the United States split up, or was it an indivisible nation?

When the North won the war, it settled the slavery and secession issues. Yes, the United States *is* one nation. It cannot be divided. States cannot pull out because they dislike how the White House runs things. The war settled the matters—but at a horrific cost. It killed at least 625,000 people. The war destroyed the South's infrastructure and economy, and it left the country drowning in debt.

How Were the Early Abolitionists Agents of Change?

The abolitionist movement was a group of people who worked to change how folks thought about slavery. In colonial days, many Americans considered it a "necessary evil." The abolitionists tried to educate Americans about the horrors of slavery. No evil is necessary. There is always another path.

- **Thomas Jefferson (1743-1826)** wrote the Declaration of Independence and was America's third president. He expressed "radical" views about slavery even before the American Revolution: "It's moral depravity and a hideous blot on our nation!" "It's contrary to the laws of nature! Everyone has the right to personal freedom." "Slavery is the greatest threat to America's survival."

  Unfortunately, Jefferson did not practice what he preached. He owned over six hundred enslaved people. After his wife died, Jefferson began a sexual relationship with his slave, Sally Hemmings, when she was about sixteen. Sally was his wife's half-sister. They had the same father, but Sally's mother was enslaved. Jefferson was the father of Sally's seven children. He freed some of them in his lifetime and left instructions in his will to free the rest after he died.

  To his credit, Jefferson legally ended slave traders bringing new enslaved people to America. In 1807, when Jefferson was president, Congress passed a national ban on importing slaves. (They still got smuggled in illegally.) But what about the enslaved people already in America? Jefferson recommended all slaves should be educated, released as adults, and sent to a colony in Africa.

- **Ralph Waldo Emerson (1803-82)** was a philosopher and poet in the transcendentalist movement popular in the 1800s. This movement taught that people and nature are good at their core but corrupted by society. They believed that one's intuition or gut feelings are more important than what one sees and experiences in real life.

Emerson gave lectures opposing slavery and spoke out against the ***Fugitive Slave Law***, which said that an enslaved person who escaped and traveled to another state had to be returned. In his 1860 essay collection, *The Conduct of Life*, Emerson said that civil war might be the only way to end slavery. He roared out in a speech, "The South calls slavery an institution ... I call it destitution."

Although he influenced people against slavery in his speeches and essays, Emerson believed in a hierarchy of races (common at that time and eventually part of Nazi philosophy). He believed those of European descent were better than Africans, and, among Europeans, the Saxons (Germanic people in England and Germany) were superior.

Frederick Douglass[18]

- **Frederick Douglass (1818-95)** was an enslaved Black person in Maryland who escaped to New York when he was about twenty. "A new world had opened upon me. If life is more than breath and the 'quick round of blood,' I lived more in one day than in a year of my slave life. It was a time of joyous excitement which words can but tamely describe."

  Douglass had learned to read and write while an enslaved person and taught other enslaved men to read. When he escaped slavery, he became a preacher. Once, while speaking against slavery in Indiana, a mob attacked him and broke his hand. Douglass changed his name after escaping slavery but was always looking over his shoulder, wondering if his former owner would hunt him down. He traveled to Ireland and England, speaking in churches. Some British friends legally bought his freedom from his owner.

  Douglass returned to New York state and began publishing an anti-slavery newspaper, *North Star*. He and his wife also worked with the Underground Railroad, assisting escaped slaves on their way to freedom in Canada. Although the Northern states did not have slaves, the Fugitive Slave Law required the Northern states to return slaves to their masters in the Southern states.

  After the Civil War, Douglass strongly advocated for Black men to have the right to vote. (Neither White nor Black women could vote until 1919.) He started the first Black labor union in the United States: the *American League of Colored Laborers*.

How Did the Second Great Awakening Influence the Abolition Movement?

In 1803, the Louisiana Purchase doubled America's land area. The United States bought 828,000 square miles of land west of the Mississippi from France. A surge of nearly one million pioneers poured into the new frontier. Several years before this happened, Christian ministers had been moaning about the spiritual need in Kentucky and Tennessee, where many of these pioneers came from. They said, "Most of them have never seen a Bible, much less read one. Thousands out here have never been baptized or heard a sermon! They've never heard the name of Christ except in curses."

New territory from the Louisiana Purchase[19]

The spiritual condition of the settlers seemed hopeless until reports began filtering in of "times of refreshing." It started with several Presbyterian ministers in Kentucky and Tennessee, led by Rev. James McGready, who began holding camp meetings. As the ministers preached, many people fell to the ground, shrieking in anguish, "How can I be saved?" God's love and goodness overwhelmed them as they responded to the call for salvation.

The revival spread from Kentucky and Tennessee into Indiana and Ohio, and the Methodist and Baptist churches joined in. Renewed faith followed the pioneers into the Midwest. In the Northeast, a revival occurred at Yale University, under its new president, Timothy Dwight (Jonathan Edwards' grandson), and spread through the New England colleges.

Some pastors had already been preaching against slavery. The Quakers had always spoken out against the unjust system. Now, the new religious fervor among evangelicals amplified the message: "All people bear the image of our Creator! That means we are all equal."

Renewed faith led to a desire to cure problems in society, like alcoholism, prostitution, and child labor. Devout men and women took up the cause of slavery. Most abolitionists were in the Northern states, which had already outlawed slavery. They shamed the Southern churchgoers, "It's hypocritical to say you're a Christian when you own slaves!"

What Part Did the Democrat and Republican Parties Play?

A question arose about the territory from the Louisiana Purchase. Would slavery be allowed in the new Midwestern states? The Democratic Party was formed in 1828 as a pro-slavery party. The Republican Party was established in 1854 and opposed expanding slavery to new territories. The two parties clashed over the **Kansas-Nebraska Act** of 1854, which the Democrats drafted and President Franklin Pierce signed.

The Kansas-Nebraska Act permitted the opening of new land for American settlers and the building of a transcontinental railroad through it. However, in politics, it's always a game of "If you sign my bill, I promise I'll do such and such for you." To get the Southern Democrats to support the Kansas-Nebraska Act, the backers promised to repeal the **Missouri Compromise** of 1820.

The Missouri Compromise did three things. It admitted Maine and Missouri into the US as new states. It said that Maine was a free state but that Missouri could have slaves. However, aside from Missouri, the bill said there could be no new slave states north of latitude 36°30' north. The backers of the Kansas-Nebraska Act got the Missouri Compromise overturned. Now, the Northern states in the new territory could have slaves.

How Did Abraham Lincoln's Election Shake Things Up?

For the 1860 presidential elections, the Republicans chose Abraham Lincoln as their candidate. He made a campaign promise that the new territories would not have slavery. Lincoln won the election, becoming America's first Republican president. At that point, seven Southern states seceded from the United States. South Carolina left the Union first. Alabama, Florida, Georgia, Louisiana, Mississippi, and Texas withdrew two months later. The seven states formed a new country: the Confederate States of America. Arkansas, North Carolina, Tennessee, and Virginia seceded within several months. In February, the Confederates elected Jefferson Davis as their president. He had been secretary of war and a United States senator.

At the beginning of the Civil War [20]

Lincoln's government and the Northern states refused to recognize the Confederate States. On April 12, 1861, events at Fort Sumter near Charleston triggered war. The Confederates took control of the fort and lowered the American flag. Insurrection! President Lincoln called out for his army. Over the next four years, almost three million soldiers confronted each other in battle. Families were split, with some men fighting for the North and other brothers or sons for the South.

What Resources and Leadership Did Each Side Have?

At the beginning of the war, the population in the North (around 22 million) was more than twice that of the South. Of the South's nine million people, four million were enslaved. The North also had more resources, like food, money, and factories. Yet, the Confederates held a vast swathe of land with excellent ports. Making headway in the Southern states spread the Union army thin.

Two important generals were Robert E. Lee and Ulysses S. Grant. Both graduated from the United States Military Academy at West Point. Lee came from one of Virginia's founding families and became the Confederates' lead commander. Grant commanded the Northern troops and was elected President of the United States after the war. The two men had different leadership styles but became seasoned and stellar commanders as the war continued.

Battle of Bull Run, Virginia, July 1861

The first major confrontation was the Battle of Bull Run, only twenty-five miles from Washington, D.C. Before the battle started, both sides were confident that they would win the war quickly. After the brutal and bloody encounter of more than sixty thousand men, both sides realized there would be no quick and easy win. Nevertheless, no one imagined the struggle would last four years.

The battle began at dawn when Union General Irvin McDowell led his troops up Bull Run Creek. He hoped to cross behind General P. G. T. Beauregard's rebel forces. However, the Confederate scouts spotted them, and McDowell lost the element of surprise. Nevertheless, his men successfully pushed the rebels into retreat. But then, Brig. Gen. Thomas J. Jackson arrived with a Virginia brigade.

Jackson earned the nickname "Stonewall" that day. His men hid in the tall grass on a hill. Not knowing they were there, McDowell positioned his rifled artillery batteries just three hundred yards away. They were sitting ducks for Stonewall's men. Jackson's men held the line like a "stone wall" until Confederate reinforcements arrived and chased the Union soldiers down the hill.

Crowds of spectators had come from D.C. to watch the battle, confident the Union would crush the rebels. As the Union soldiers rushed in full retreat, they collided with the spectators. Almost three thousand Union soldiers were killed, wounded, or captured compared to about two thousand Confederates.

The Thai King Offers His War Elephants

In early 1861, Rama IV of Siam offered to ship some war elephants to America. "I heard you have no elephants! I would like to send you several pairs. You can set them loose in your forests to breed and build up large herds. With their enormous size and strength, they can easily travel through uncleared woods and matted jungles." Abraham Lincoln wrote back, politely thanking the king for his kind offer but explaining that America's climate and geography did not favor breeding elephants.

Battle of Antietam, September 1862

This battle had horrifying casualties (22,000). And yet, the blood bath had no clear winner. Lincoln declared a Union win, but the North lost more men. What's worse, Union General George B. McClellan dropped the ball tactically. He wasn't aggressive enough, allowing General Robert E. Lee to move his men around and fend off the Union attacks.

Lee marched into Maryland, intending to move the war to the North. He even hoped to capture Washington, D.C. Stonewall Jackson had just scored an astounding victory at Harper's Ferry, where all thirteen thousand Union soldiers surrendered. Lee lined his men up at Antietam Creek. It was too deep and swift to cross except by bridge. His men could fire on the Union soldiers without worrying about a charge.

However, General McClellan sent part of his Union army downstream to cross over a bridge. They hiked back on the other side of the river and attacked the Confederates' left flank in a cornfield. However, Jackson's men mowed down the Union soldiers in the field and held the line. Other Union soldiers crossed the creek and attacked the center forces, yet they could not hold the charge. They retreated. The Union General Ambrose Burnside crossed another bridge under heavy fire. He attacked the Confederate right flank and would have won, except more Confederate men arrived from Harper's Ferry and saved the day.

So many men suffered horrific injuries that the battlefield doctors were overwhelmed. Nurse Clara Barton (who later founded the Red Cross) arrived with a wagon full of bandages and other medical supplies. The "Angel of the Battlefield" assisted the surgeons in caring for the injured and dying men as the bullets were still flying.

Clara Barton, Founder of the Red Cross [21]

Emancipation Proclamation, 1863

On New Year's Day, 1863, Abraham Lincoln's Emancipation Proclamation took effect. It freed the enslaved people in the "rebellious states" but not those in the Union. Four states in the Union —Delaware, Kentucky, Maryland, and Missouri—still had slaves. They were the border states between the North and South. Lincoln was afraid that if he made them give up their slaves, they would go over to the Confederate side.

What was the point of the Emancipation Proclamation? If the enslaved people in the Confederate states could escape to the North, they were officially free. About one-half million did, but three million stayed in the South. If enslaved men could flee to a Union army that was fighting in the South, they were considered free and could join the army. About 180,000 Black men served in the Union Army, but some had been free before the war started.

Battle of Gettysburg, Pennsylvania, July 1863

The Battle of Gettysburg turned the tide for a Union victory. Robert E. Lee made a second attempt to invade the North, hoping to score a win for the Confederates. He made it to Pennsylvania. However, losing over one-third of his men (killed, injured, or captured) dashed his hopes.

The battle began when the Union army launched a surprise attack on Confederate forces marching to Gettysburg to snatch supplies. The Confederates fended off the Union soldiers, but the following day, the Union line blocked access to Gettysburg. General Lee had more men than the Union, so he outflanked the Union army.

The South prevailed on the second day, but disaster loomed on the third day. The Confederate soldiers daringly launched a charge toward a small ridge. They reached the top and held it temporarily but lost over half their men. Lee's forces withdrew and plodded south through the rain. Inexplicably, Union General George Meade did not chase them, to President Lincoln's despair. "We had only to stretch forth our hands, and they were ours."

The War Grinds to an End

The war raged on for two more years, with around a hundred more battles and skirmishes. Both sides used submarines—or at least tried to.

The Union had a submarine called the *Alligator* with compressed air and a diver lock. However, before it was used in war, it sank in a storm off Cape Hatteras. In February 1864, the Confederate *H. L. Hunley* sank the USS *Housatonic*, the first time a submarine sank a warship. Nevertheless, the blast also killed the crew members on the *Hunley*, and it sank to the bottom of the Atlantic Ocean outside Charleston Harbor.

In May 1864, General William Sherman penetrated the Confederate heartland. For two months, he battled his way closer and closer to Atlanta. When he reached the outskirts, part of his army pummeled Atlanta with cannon fire while the rest severed the railroad lines around the city, cutting off supplies. In September, Atlanta surrendered. Sherman left Atlanta in ashes and marched from there to Savannah, leaving a swathe of destruction in his wake.

On April 9, 1865, General Lee surrendered to General Grant at the Appomattox Court House in Virginia. The war was over, although it took a few weeks for the other Confederate armies and states to surrender.

On April 14, 1865, President Lincoln was assassinated, and his vice president, Andrew Johnson, became president. Johnson granted amnesty to most of the Confederate leaders and soldiers. By December 1865, the Thirteenth Amendment passed, which ended slavery in the United States.

Roundup Activity: Essay

Choose a vital aspect of the Civil War, such as a significant battle, the abolition movement, or the results of the war. Write a half-page essay highlighting why it was important in changing American history.

Chapter 5: Civil Rights

Perhaps you are wondering why this chapter appears in the middle of the book. Wasn't the civil rights movement a 1960s thing? Yes, it was, but the struggle did not begin then. The Thirteenth Amendment ended slavery, but people of color still had limited rights. How did the struggle for equality unfold? How did civil rights heroes shatter the strongholds of segregation and discrimination? Let's explore this important topic.

What Is Racism?

Racism is the belief that a person's genetics determines their morality, intelligence, and abilities. Many people of European ancestry justified slavery because they thought Africans and Indigenous Americans were racially inferior. Did they really believe that—in their heart of hearts? For some slave owners, labeling non-Whites as "lesser" people helped them avoid a guilty conscience. Other Americans and Europeans sincerely believed the White race was superior and had every right to dominate the world.

How Did Abraham Lincoln Weigh In?

Abraham Lincoln clarified his views in his debate with Stephen A. Douglas in 1858:

"I am not, nor ever have been, in favor of bringing about in any way the social and political equality of the white and black races ... I am not nor ever have been in favor of making voters or jurors of negroes, nor of qualifying them to hold office, nor to intermarry with white people. I will say, in addition to this, that there is a physical difference between the white and black races, which I believe will forever forbid the two races living together on terms of social and political equality. And inasmuch as they cannot so live, while they do remain together, there must be the position of superior and inferior, and I as much as any other man am in favor of having the superior position assigned to the white race."[i]

However, Lincoln's views on race are complex and hotly debated. There is evidence that his views shifted over time.

How Did Charles Darwin Contribute to Racist Ideology?

In the mid-1800s, Darwin wrote about his theory of evolution. Because evolution was an ongoing process, he said that those of European descent were more evolved than those from Africa. Thus, Darwin believed that a racial hierarchy was natural. Whites should run the show because they evolved earlier and had more abilities. He even suggested in *The Descent of Man* (1871) that "the civilized races of man will almost certainly exterminate and replace the savage races throughout the world."[ii]

What Happened in the Reconstruction Period? (1863–77)

Reconstruction was the rebuilding and reshaping of the nation at the end of the Civil War. The formerly enslaved Black people were free, but what did freedom look like? What rights did they have?

President Lincoln was shot just five days after General Lee surrendered to General Grant. Before Lincoln died, the Republicans were pushing for equal rights for the freed slaves. They wanted to make that a condition for states returning to the Union. Several days before his murder, Lincoln talked about allowing some Black Americans the right

---

[i] Neely, Mark E. Jr., *The Abraham Lincoln Encyclopedia* (Da Capo Press, Inc., 1982), "Fourth Debate: Charleston, Illinois, September 18, 1858," National Park Service. https://www.nps.gov/liho/learn/historyculture/debate4.htm.

[ii] Charles Darwin, *The Descent of Man and Selection in Relation to Sex* (Classic Literature Library, 1871), 105. https://charles-darwin.classic-literature.co.uk/the-descent-of-man/ebook-page-105.asp.

to vote—if they had served in the Union Army and if they were "very intelligent."

Weeks after unexpectedly becoming president, Andrew Johnson announced the "Reconstruction Act." It spelled out how the Southern states would be readmitted into the United States.

Three new laws stated what rights the newly freed Black Americans had. The Thirteenth Amendment (December 1865) freed the enslaved people. The Fourteenth Amendment (July 1868) said everyone born in America had United States citizenship. The citizenship of African Americans had been controversial, as illustrated in the "Dred Scott Case."

Dred Scott by Louis Schultze, circa 1888[20]

Dred Scott and his wife Harriet were enslaved African Americans. Their owner, John Emerson, moved several times. They started in Missouri, a slave state. But then, Emerson moved to Illinois (a free state) and Wisconsin Territory (also free). Finally, Emerson moved back to Missouri with the Scotts. Emerson died, and the Scotts tried to buy their freedom from his wife, but she refused.

The Scotts then filed lawsuits for freedom. Technically, they were free when they lived in Illinois and Wisconsin, and the courts usually followed a "once free, always free" rule. Yet, the courts turned down the Scotts' lawsuits. The US Supreme Court said in 1857 that Dred Scott was not a citizen and that slaves were "inferior" and had no rights. One year later, the Blow family bought the Scotts from Mrs. Emerson and promptly set them free. Dred only lived a year in freedom before dying of tuberculosis, but Harriet lived until 1876.

The Fourteenth Amendment also said that the US government and the local state governments could not take away a person's life, freedom, or property without legal due process. Everyone (including formerly enslaved people) had to be equally protected by the federal and state laws. The Fifteenth Amendment (February 1870) gave Black men the right to vote.

Most Southerners were pardoned. Johnson allowed the Southern states to govern as they chose as long as they got rid of slavery and paid off their war debt. As expected, the Southern states only elected White men as leaders. They passed **Black Codes**. These laws said Black Americans had to sign annual labor contracts. Any Black people without a job were "vagrants" who could be forced to work for the White plantation owners. Life had not changed much for Southern African Americans.

What Was the Memphis Massacre? (May 1866)

Tensions were high during the Reconstruction period. After getting freed, many Black people in Tennessee left the rural plantations and moved to Memphis. The city's Black population swelled to about twenty thousand. Some Black men were already there. They had fought in the 3rd US Colored Artillery Regiment of the Union Army and now lived in and around Fort Pickering, just outside Memphis.

Many Irish people had immigrated to Memphis after the 1840s Great Famine in Ireland. The recently-arrived Irish took most of the police and firefighter jobs. The freed Africans competed with the Irish population for craftsmen and labor jobs. Tensions flared between the two groups. On May 1, 1866, the African American Veterans held a street party celebrating the war's end by shooting their guns in the air. The (mostly Irish) police tried to break up the party, but the African Americans refused because they were outside Memphis police jurisdiction.

SCENES IN MEMPHIS, TENNESSEE, DURING THE RIOT—BURNING A FREEDMEN'S SCHOOL-HOUSE.
[SKETCHED BY A. R. W.]

Freedmen's Schoolhouse burns in the 1866 Memphis Riot in this illustration by Alfred Rudolph Waud, Harper's Weekly.[28]

A police officer reached for his gun but accidentally shot himself in the leg. His companions thought the Black soldiers had shot him. In the chaos, bullets flew, and a police officer was killed. As a mob formed, General Stoneman sent two units of soldiers to disperse the mob and ordered the Black veterans to come inside the fort. By 11 p.m., everything was quiet around Fort Pickering.

Yet, the mob (which was one-third policemen and firefighters) wanted revenge. They couldn't get to the Black soldiers, so they turned on the African American neighborhoods in Memphis. They burned down Black schools, twelve churches, and ninety-one homes, some with people still in them. They killed forty-six Black people and injured countless others.

The New Orleans Massacre, July 1866

Three months after the Memphis atrocities, another bloodbath ensued in New Orleans. The Democrats were trying to regain power and keep the Black people "in their place." The Republicans were holding their local convention at the New Orleans Mechanics Institute, promoting the right of Black people to vote. About two hundred unarmed Black veterans marched in a parade to the convention.

Suddenly, a horde of police officers, firemen, and armed Democrats descended on the parade. They kicked and clubbed the African Americans, then turned on the Republicans in the institute, firing into the windows. The unarmed people inside desperately tried to escape, slipping on the blood-covered floor. Thirty-seven unarmed people died, and over one hundred suffered severe injuries.

How Did "Redemption" Impact Black Americans?

"The slave went free, stood a brief moment in the sun, then moved back again toward slavery."[1]

The "Redeemers" were Southern White Democrats retaliating against the gains made on behalf of formerly enslaved Americans. The Redeemers called any White people who advocated for Black Americans "Scalawags." Former Confederate soldiers created the Ku Klux Klan, a terrorist group targeting Black Americans, Jews, and Catholics. Wearing hooded white robes, they burned crosses in front of Black leaders' homes. They lynched (murdered by hanging) over three thousand Black people and more than one thousand White people who supported civil rights.

---

[1] W. E. B. Du Bois, an African American historian and civil rights activist. https://duboiscenter.library.umass.edu/du-bois-quotes/.

A Ku Klux Klan demonstration in Tampa, Florida, 1939[94]

The Southern Democrats worked to overturn Black people's right to vote despite it now being constitutional. People who registered to vote had to pay poll taxes, which many African Americans could not afford. Another requirement was a literacy test. For instance, a person might have to read a paragraph of the state constitution and interpret it. Many enslaved people had never learned to read. Even if they could read, the registration officials subjectively decided whether or not they passed. The poll tax and literacy requirements cut the Black voters by more than half.

"Jim Crow" laws lasting into the 1970s were another method of "keeping down" Black people in the South. Many restaurants made Black patrons eat outside. Blacks and Whites had separate schools, railroad cars, hospitals, water fountains, restrooms, and parks. African Americans had to sit at the back of the bus.

How Did the "Great Migration" Shift America's Black Population? (1916-70)

Life was nearly unbearable for Black people in the South. They had few opportunities to get ahead in life. More than six million Black Americans moved to the West, Midwest, and especially to the North in the early and mid-1900s. Industry was taking off in the North, and recruiters passed through Southern towns, offering good pay for work in Northern factories.

Even in the North, African Americans encountered racism. City maps had "red lines" that marked Black neighborhoods. These were the only places where African Americans could get a home loan. It meant that schools were essentially segregated. This practice continued well into the 1960s. However, the African Americans who moved north could register to vote without the nonsense of poll taxes and reading tests. This gave them a political voice and elevated many Black people into leadership positions.

Antisemitism in America

Black Americans were not the only victims of racism. As deadly antisemitism ramped up in Europe in the late 1800s and early 1900s, millions of Jews immigrated to America. Even in America, Jews experienced racist policies. For instance, schools like Harvard, Yale, and Princeton had quotas for how many Jewish students could enroll. Some colleges banned Jews altogether.

The American industrialist Henry Ford published a newspaper called the *Dearborn*, which was full of antisemitic propaganda. He and many other Americans feared the Jews would use their business genius to take over the world. Of course, Hitler's manifesto, *Mein Kampf*, fueled the fire. American radio stations freely aired Nazi ideas and hatred against Jews. Vandals painted swastikas on Jewish businesses.

The American government had quotas on how many Jewish immigrants were allowed. They sent hundreds back to Germany and the Holocaust, which killed six million Jews.

After World War II, the atrocities observed and photographed in Hitler's concentration camps by American troops jarred the American public. Americans began to sympathize with the plight of the Jews. Restrictions and quotas faded away. As they were permitted to move ahead in life, Jewish Americans won an astounding number of Nobel prizes. Yet, even today, antisemitism continues, especially on America's college campuses.

Rosa Parks and the Montgomery Bus Boycott (1955-56)

In 1955, Mrs. Rosa Parks got on the bus to go home. She was weary after a long day at work. In Montgomery, Alabama, the Jim Crow laws said Black folks had to sit in the back of the bus. Mrs. Parks sat down in the first row of the Black people's section. However, the White people's section in the front filled up. The bus driver told Rosa to move further back so White people could sit in her seat.

However, Mrs. Rosa Parks was tired of all the rules Black people had to endure to "keep them in their place." Earlier that week, she had attended a meeting at Dexter Avenue Baptist Church, pastored by Rev. Martin Luther King, Jr. Everyone was talking about Emmett Till, a fourteen-year-old in Mississippi. Someone said he had flirted with a White woman. He'd been kidnapped, blinded, beaten, shot, and thrown into the Tallahatchie River. The all-White jury said his murderers were "not guilty," and they walked free.

The bus driver cleared his throat. "Move to the back!"

Rosa quietly said, "No."

As his face turned red, the driver had Mrs. Parks arrested. Reverend King helped bail her out, and then he and his friend, Ralph Abernathy, planned a bus boycott. They spread leaflets from door to door in the Black community and churches that read "Don't ride the bus on Monday!" Most African Americans in the South did not own cars. The leaflets suggested they walk to work, share rides, or take a cab.

Rosa Parks arrested a second time in 1956 for helping organize the bus boycott[35]

That Monday, it rained. Nevertheless, only eight Black people rode the bus. Everyone else carpooled, biked, took a cab, or walked. And not just Monday—they boycotted Montgomery's bus system for an entire year! Since at least half of Montgomery's bus riders were African Americans, the bus company went bankrupt. The police arrested Reverend King and even the carpool drivers for "interfering with a business." Racist thugs bombed four African American churches and Reverend King's house.

Many angry Black Americans wanted to strike back. Some civil rights activists, like Malcolm X, advocated for a violent revolution. But Reverend King insisted, "We meet violence with non-violence. We meet hate with love. Jesus told us to love our enemies and pray for them."

Finally, victory was achieved! The courts said it was unconstitutional to segregate the buses. The state appealed, and it went to the Supreme Court, which ruled that buses could not be segregated.

Martin Luther King Jr.

After winning the case against segregated buses, Rev. Martin Luther King Jr. continued advocating for equality for African Americans. In 1963, he gave his famous "I Have a Dream" speech in Washington, D.C.:

> "Now is the time to make real the promises of democracy. Now is the time to rise from the dark and desolate valley of segregation to the sunlit path of racial justice. Now is the time to lift our nation from the quicksands of racial injustice to the solid rock of brotherhood. Now is the time to make justice a reality for all of God's children."[i]

As Martin Luther King Jr. and other activists like Malcolm X pushed for civil rights in the early 1960s, they found sympathetic allies in President Kennedy and President Johnson. American attitudes slowly began to shift. New laws were passed to protect African Americans' rights. For instance, the 1964 Civil Rights Act banned racial and gender discrimination against employees. That same year, King won the Nobel Peace Prize. The 1965 Voting Rights Act eliminated the poll taxes. Segregated schools, buses, and restrooms became a thing of the past. Sadly, King's untiring work generated enemies. In 1968, he was shot and

---

[i] Martin Luther King Jr., "'I Have a Dream' Speech." *History.* November 30, 2017. https://www.history.com/topics/black-history/i-have-a-dream-speech.

killed in Tennessee. Days later, the Fair Housing Act was passed. It banned housing discrimination due to national origin, race, religion, or gender.

Martin Luther King Jr. giving his "I Have a Dream" speech [36]

The "Post-racial" Era

America celebrated Barack Obama's election as president in 2009 as a monumental milestone for civil rights. Nevertheless, the struggle continues. African American men are three times more likely to be killed by police than White men. The poverty rate for Black people in 2023 was 17.9 percent compared to 7.7 percent for White people. Black babies are twice as likely to die as White babies. From a legal perspective, everyone has equal rights. Yet, in real life, America has a long journey.

Roundup Activity: Multiple Choice

Check your answers in the back of the book.

1. Which of the following did Abraham Lincoln believe about Black people?

   a. They could serve on juries.

   b. They could hold political office.

   c. They could marry White people.

   d. None of the above

2. Which of the following did Charles Darwin believe about White people?

   a. They were more evolved than people from Africa.

   b. Because White people evolved earlier, they should be in control.

   c. The civilized races would replace the savage races.

   d. All of the above

3. Dred Scott lost his court case for freedom because...

   a. The court ignored the "once free, always free" rule.

   b. The court said he was not a citizen.

   c. The court said he was an "inferior" slave with no rights.

   d. All of the above

4. Who got called "Scalawags" ?

   a. Southern Democrats trying to keep Black people down.

   b. Formerly enslaved Black people.

   c. White people who advocated for formerly enslaved Blacks.

   d. All of the above

5. How did some White people retaliate against the bus boycott by Black people?

   a. The police arrested Martin Luther King Jr. and the carpool drivers.

   b. Racists bombed four Black churches.

   c. Racists bombed King's house.

   d. All of the above

Chapter 6: The War Against the World

The early twentieth century saw America dragged into two worldwide conflicts. World War I, which killed at least sixteen million people, was supposed to be the "war to end all wars." Yet, two decades later, World War II erupted as the bloodiest war in world history. America played a leading and decisive role in both. The collisions of nations placed America as the world's superpower—yet it came at a crushing cost.

World War I (1914-18)

World War I was horrific. The world had never seen a war involving so many countries. It raged between the Central Powers (Austria-Hungary, Germany, and the Ottoman Empire) and the Allied Powers (Britain, France, and Russia). Eventually, the United States got sucked in and fought for the Allied side. Before it ended, over thirty countries were fighting. Most battles were in Europe, where a regional conflict snowballed into a war encircling the globe.

What Triggered the War?

It all started in Sarajevo, the capital of Bosnia, a country in the Austro-Hungarian Empire. The Serbs were a Slavic ethnic group. Most lived in Serbia, next to Bosnia. Some lived in Bosnia and wanted independence from the Austro-Hungarian Empire. In June 1914, a teenage Serb shot and killed Archduke Franz Ferdinand and his wife Sophie. Ferdinand was the nephew of Austria-Hungary's emperor. He was supposed to be the next emperor.

"You plotted against my heir!" the emperor cried, declaring war on Serbia. Complicated alliances dragged most of Europe into the conflict. Russia and France supported Serbia, so Austria-Hungary invaded Russia. Germany supported Austria-Hungary, so it declared war on France. Luxembourg and Belgium were neutral, but they were in the way, so Germany invaded them to get to France. British troops arrived in France to defend their ally against Germany.

Map of Europe just before WWI began[27]

Within months, four hundred miles of trenches called the "Western Front" stretched through France near its borders with Belgium and Germany. Japan and Australia joined the Allies. Bulgaria and the Ottoman Empire, which controlled much of the Middle East, jumped in with Germany and Austria-Hungary (the Central Powers). In May 1915, Italy joined the Allies, although it had previously partnered with Germany and Austria-Hungary.

How Did the US Get Involved?

For three years, the United States remained neutral, even after the Germans torpedoed the *Lusitania* in 1915. It was the world's largest passenger ship, on its way from New York to England. By sinking it, the Germans killed 1,197 people, including 128 Americans. However, the

Lusitania was a British ship. President Wilson threatened Germany with war if they sank any American ships.

German submarines continued to prowl the seas, endangering shipping. On January 31, 1917, the Germans announced that they would attack every ship in the Mediterranean or near Britain and France. That's exactly what they did. In the next two months, they sank nine American ships flying under a neutral flag. America declared war on Germany on April 6, 1917, believing it was necessary for world peace and safe shipping.

Engraving of the Lusitania sinking by Norman Wilkinson, The Illustrated London News[98]

Once the US joined the Allies, Cuba, Greece, and China joined, followed by Nicaragua, Costa Rica, Haiti, and Honduras. The Allies breathed a sigh of relief. Many British soldiers were dead, wounded, or extremely exhausted. Half the surviving French soldiers were on strike, demoralized after losing the Second Battle of the Aisne. Meanwhile, Russia was in the middle of a violent revolution. The Marxist Bolsheviks, led by Vladimir Lenin, came to power and pulled out of the war.

What Was Different About This War?

Never before had so many nations been in the same war. Almost five million American soldiers fought. Meanwhile, women stepped into the men's places in factories and farms, doubling the female employment rate. Twenty-one thousand American women were nurses in the army, and thousands of "Hello Girls" worked as switchboard operators near the front lines. The navy recruited women as translators, radio operators, and truck drivers, freeing up men for combat.

A WWI recruitment poster for women[39]

World War I saw mind-blowing innovations in weapons, technology, manufacturing, and communications. Tanks were used for the first time, and WWI began the race for air supremacy. Machine guns were used for the first time on military airplanes in WWI and became a key weapon. Each US regiment had 336 machine guns by the war's end.

What Were Some Decisive Battles for the American Military?

America's first battle was at **Cantigny (May 1918)** in northern France. The French provided logistics, flamethrowers, and tanks. The US First Infantry Division's goal was to take the village of Cantigny. They did that in a half hour and captured 250 German soldiers. However, the Germans counterattacked the next day. They killed or wounded eight hundred American soldiers before abandoning the area.

In **June 1918**, the US 4th Marine Brigade joined French and British forces in the **Battle of Belleau Wood,** about one hundred miles east of Paris. This was the first large-scale battle for the US Marine Corps. The French ordered the US Marines to drop back and dig trenches as the Germans advanced through the woods. Instead, the Marine Corps commander ordered his men to hold their position and not open fire until the Germans were a hundred yards away. The hail of bullets killed many Germans, and they retreated. The next day, the Marines engaged in hand-to-hand combat in the thick woods. The Nazis killed or injured over one thousand Marines that day. But the tenacious Marines kept fighting for three weeks and finally chased the Germans away.

The **Hundred Days Offensive (August–November 1918)** was a series of battles along the Western Front in France. In one battle, a half million Americans and a hundred thousand French soldiers took back Saint-Mihiel. This was a stellar win because Germany had held the fortified town for four years.

At the Meuse-Argonne Offensive, one million American soldiers pushed the Germans forty miles back. Over 26,000 US troops died in America's most colossal battle in military history.

World War I trench warfare[80]

America's stunning victory at the Meuse-Argonne ended the war. Germany signed an armistice on November 11, 1918. The allies met in Paris in January 1919 to negotiate the *Treaty of Versailles*. They formed the *League of Nations,* a forum to resolve international disputes. Although America was in the war for less than six months, 53,402 US soldiers died in battle. Another 63,114 died from disease and accidents. The European Allies and Central Powers suffered far worse.

What happened to the Serbs in Bosnia—the ones who started the war? They won independence. The Austro-Hungarian Empire dissolved. Bosnia, Serbia, and other Slavic people formed the Kingdom of Serbs, Croats, and Slovenes (later Yugoslavia).

World War II (1939–45)

Nazi Germany's invasion of Poland triggered the Second World War, entangling nations around the globe in shocking violence. Once again, America tried to stay out of the war, but Japan's surprise attack changed everything. World War II killed over fifty million people and unleashed the atomic bomb. As the war ended, the horrified world learned of Hitler's Holocaust, which systematically murdered six million Jews.

Why Did America Get Involved This Time Around?

Most Americans preferred to sit this war out. It had only been two decades since the horrors of WWI. America was pulling out of the *Great Depression (1929-39)*, a dreadful time when the economy collapsed and unemployment skyrocketed. Congress wanted to continue an *isolationist*, neutral position. They did not want to get involved in other people's fights.

However, in May and June 1940, Hitler's military swallowed up Belgium, the Netherlands, and part of France. What's worse, Hitler forged a fascist alliance with the Italian dictator Mussolini, planning to conquer Britain.

Fascism promotes a country's strength over its people's welfare. People living in fascist countries have few freedoms and face persecution if they criticize the government. Fascist leaders are usually violent dictators with unlimited power. They usually believe in a social hierarchy, the idea that some people are better than others. Hitler believed that the Germanic ethnicity was so superior that it had the right to rule the world and that Jews had no right to exist.

The Nazis were bombing London and torpedoing British ships. Would Hitler and Mussolini take over all of Europe? In addition, Japan wanted Southeast Asia's Dutch, French, and British colonies. Germany, Japan, and Italy signed the ***Tripartite Pact*** in September 1940. The ***Axis*** powers pledged that if the United States attacked any of their three countries, the other two would defend them.

President Roosevelt still refused to join the war. However, he sent weapons to Britain. The US Navy escorted British merchant ships in convoys, protecting them from German attack. When Japan invaded Indochina, America cut off oil going to Japan.

Japan Attacks Pearl Harbor

Hitler wanted to avoid war with America, at least for the time being. He planned to conquer the Soviet Union first. However, Japan had other ideas. The Japanese wanted to control oil-rich Southeast Asia and did not want interference from the US military bases in Hawaii and the Philippines.

On December 7, 1941, the Japanese staged a surprise attack on Pearl Harbor, the American naval base in Hawaii. They sank four American battleships and damaged the other four in port. They took out eight other military ships and almost two hundred aircraft. The Japanese killed 2,393 Americans and wounded 1,178. It was the most lethal foreign attack on American soil up to that point.

The destroyer USS Shaw explodes from Japanese bombs at Pearl Harbor.[81]

Japan's reckless action enraged America. Now, everyone was up in arms and wanted revenge. President Roosevelt declared war against Japan the next day, December 8. Germany and Italy declared war against the United States three days later.

The Soviet Union knew it was in Hitler's crosshairs. Consequently, the Communists formed an unlikely union with Britain and America. The Chinese were already fighting Japan and decided that "the enemy of your enemy is your friend." China joined America, Britain, and the Soviet Union, forming the ***Allied Big Four***. With twenty-two other countries, they signed a formal treaty called the ***United Nations Declaration***.

Fighting on Two Fronts

America faced off against Japan, Germany, and Italy in its new global war. This forced it to fight in Asia and Europe at the same time. The United States sent food, weapons, tanks, and aircraft to the Soviet Union, which fought bravely against Germany and, later, Japan. It cost the Soviets twenty-seven million lives. Britain fought primarily in Europe, moving against Japan near the war's end.

China had been in the middle of a civil war between the Nationalist Party and the Communist Party. They stopped fighting each other and started fighting their mutual enemy when Japan invaded in 1937. The Chinese suffered horrible atrocities at the hands of the Japanese—war crimes they have not forgiven to this day. In the *Nanjing Massacre*, the Japanese killed 200,000 civilians and raped 20,000 women and children. At least fourteen million Chinese died in World War II.

America did not have a large standing army at this time. All men under age sixty-five had to register for the draft; however, most WWII soldiers were in their teens and twenties. Over sixteen million soldiers served in the US Army, Navy, and Marines during the war. More than 350,000 women joined America's armed forces, mostly in non-combat roles.

We Can Do It!

America had to quickly produce weapons, aircraft, tanks, ships, and uniforms. Three million women flocked to the factories and shipyards to do their part for the war effort. Recruitment posters featuring "Rosie the Riveter" became iconic. Teenagers and older men also rushed to work.

America no longer had an unemployment problem. Factories ran around the clock with three shifts a day, seven days a week. In 1944, America produced over ninety thousand aircraft.

A recruitment poster by the War Production Board[33]

With many farmers at war and America helping feed the Soviet Union and Britain, civilians began growing their own vegetables and fruit in "Victory Gardens." People could only buy a small amount of coffee, sugar, and meat. With food rations, leftovers became a patriotic meal. The war effort demanded metal, so Americans scavenged their attics, basements, and yards for old mattress frames, pipes, pots, and junk cars. Carpools reduced the need for new tires so that rubber could go to military jeeps, tanks, and airplanes. Before the war, most Americans were exempt from income tax—only eight million paid taxes. Taxes increased to pay for the war. By 1945, most working adults paid income taxes.

Defeat the Nazis First!

President Franklin Roosevelt and his Joint Chiefs of Staff prioritized Europe. Their strategy was to defeat Hitler and then go after Japan.

Nevertheless, they did not neglect Asia. Admiral Chester W. Nimitz was based in Hawaii and was Commander in Chief of the Pacific area. A submarine genius, he developed *underway replenishment (UNREP) techniques*, where weapons, food, and fuel are transferred from one ship to another at sea. Warships and submarines could stay out at sea, no longer needing to enter a port.

Battle of Midway (June 1942)

Six months after Japan bombed Pearl Harbor, the Japanese Navy attacked the US Navy fleet near the tiny island of Midway, about a thousand miles from Hawaii's main islands. Luckily, the US picked up the Japanese attack plans while monitoring signals, so the Americans plotted an ambush. The American forces were ready and waiting with 344 fighters, bombers, and patrol planes, three aircraft carriers, and the USS *Nautilus* submarine. The Japanese had 248 fighter planes and four aircraft carriers.

The Americans sunk all four Japanese aircraft carriers, along with 140 airplanes still on the carriers when they sank. They shot forty-eight more Japanese planes out of the sky. With no aircraft carriers to land on, some Japanese planes ditched at sea. Others flew to Midway, wishing they had not bombed the airfield earlier. One American aircraft carrier, the *Yorktown*, sank. The US lost 144 airplanes. Over 3,000 Japanese died, compared to 307 Americans. It was "the most stunning and decisive blow in the history of naval warfare," according to military historian John Keegan.[i]

D-Day, Battle of Normandy, France (June 1944)

The stakes for winning the Battle of Normandy were high. It was history's most extensive air, land, and sea invasion. The goal was to get a foothold in the European mainland so the Allies could retake it.

The English Channel lay between Britain and France. Hitler had built his "Atlantic Wall" along the channel's coast to prevent a British invasion on the beaches. However, now that America was in the war, the Allies had more resources and manpower to cross the channel and retake Europe.

---

[i] John Keegan, *The Second World War* (Penguin Press, 2005), 275.

The Allies planned for five thousand landing boats to approach five beaches spread over fifty miles. Eleven thousand aircraft carried paratroopers and supported the land invasion. In the early morning of June 6, while it was still dark, twenty thousand American and British paratroopers floated down from the sky, landing behind enemy lines.

Wading to shore on D-Day[38]

At 5:30 a.m., waves of landing craft sailed up to the beach with 130,000 troops. They jumped into frigid, waist-high water. Struggling against a strong undertow, they waded to shore, holding their guns. Enemy fire peppered the beach and water. Once they reached the beach, they had to climb hundred-foot cliffs. By sunset, the Allies had breached Hitler's Atlantic Wall, although over ten thousand men were killed or wounded. This was a pivotal moment in the war in Europe.

Deaths of Mussolini and Hitler (April 1945)

After D-Day, the Allies took most of Europe in less than a year. In April 1945, the Soviets, led by Joseph Stalin, invaded the Nazi capital of Berlin, Germany. Hitler holed up in a bunker in the center of the city. As the Soviets closed in, Hitler received word that the Allies had killed Mussolini in Italy. Two days later, on April 30, Hitler committed suicide. The war in Europe was over.

Uncovering the Holocaust

As the Allies penetrated Germany, they found unimaginable horrors—the Nazi concentration camps. Reports had trickled out of the Nazi atrocities against Jews in Europe, but few realized how bad it was. Some American officials knew but did not care, as antisemitism was strong in America at the time. American officials in the Department of State blocked assistance for Jewish refugees and covered up intelligence reports of the Holocaust, saying "It's just a war rumor."[i]

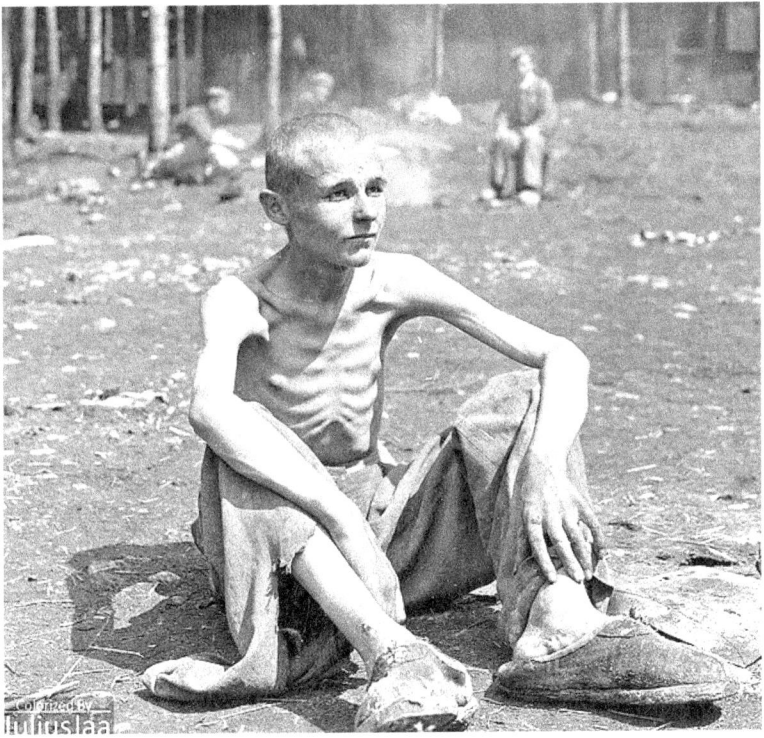

A teenager rescued from Ebensee Concentration Camp in Austria[54]

In April 1945, American soldiers were eyewitnesses to the gruesome savagery of the Nazi concentration camps. "I saw walking dead people," one soldier reported. Men, women, and teens were nothing but skin and bone, their skin covered with sores. Six million Jews, including one

---

[i] "Americans and the Holocaust." United States Holocaust Memorial Museum, Accessed January 4, 2025, https://exhibitions.ushmm.org/americans-and-the-holocaust/main/state-department-obstruction-1#:~:text=In%20early%201943%2C%20US%20State,from%20reaching%20the%20United%20States.

million children, died in the Nazi Holocaust. Hitler's troops killed five million other people. His killing machine heartlessly murdered babies, children, and adults with Down syndrome and other disabilities. The mentally ill and political prisoners were also victims.

The Atomic Bomb Explodes (August 1945)

When the Italians and Germans surrendered, Japan lost its allies. On July 26, 1945, the Allies issued the ***Potsdam Declaration***, demanding Japan's immediate surrender. What if they refused? "Prompt and utter destruction," the Allies warned. Japan made the fatal mistake of ignoring the warning.

For months, American planes had dropped sixty-three million leaflets across Japan, warning the citizens to leave the cities. On August 6, 1945, an American B-29 bomber released "Little Boy," a nuclear bomb, on Hiroshima, Japan. It killed seventy thousand people instantly. Another thirty thousand died within months from radiation sickness. Inconceivably, the Japanese continued fighting. Three days later, another nuclear bomb called "Fat Boy" dropped on Nagasaki, killing at least forty thousand. The two bombs were the only atomic weapons ever deployed in war. On August 14, Emperor Hirohito announced his surrender. The war was over.

Fat Boy detonates at Nagasaki[86]

Roundup Activity: Crossword

Crossword Puzzle: World Wars I and II

Down:
2. not getting involved in other nation's fights
3. staged a surprise attack on Pearl Harbor
4. the side America fought on in WWI
8. where America won a decisive sea battle against Japan
10. where WWI started

Across:
1. American admiral in Pacific during WWII
5. where Nazi Germany's invasion triggered WWII
6. union of Germany, Japan, and Italy against Allies
7. the city where America dropped the first atomic bomb
9. violent dictators with unlimited powers
11. where the Japanese killed 200,000 civilians
12. the war to end all wars
13. America's first WWI battle in France
14. the systematic murder of 6 million jews

Image source[86]

Chapter 7: The Space Race and the Cuban Issue

The United States's relationship with its former allies, Cuba and the Soviet Union, grew icy during the Cold War. They were on opposite sides of the political ideology fence. Russia's revolution in 1917, led by Lenin's Bolshevik Party, overthrew the tsar and set up the world's first Communist government. In 1922, it formed the Union of Soviet Socialist Republics (USSR). Its empire grew to include fifteen states and achieved superpower status in World War II. At its peak, the Soviet Union was the largest nation on earth, covering one-sixth of the planet.

What Was the Cold War?

After World War II, America and its European allies grew increasingly nervous about the Soviet Union. Could the USSR take over all of Europe? Could it even control the entire earth? In 1949, America joined with Canada and twelve European allies to form **NATO**—the *North Atlantic Treaty Organization*. It was (and still is) a military alliance where the members pledged to defend each other from attack by a third party.

The most problematic third party was the Soviet Union. The USSR struck back in 1955 by forming the **Warsaw Pact** with **Eastern Bloc** countries. The Eastern Bloc nations embraced the Communist politics of the USSR. These two alliances—NATO and the Warsaw Pact—set off the **Cold War**. This power struggle persisted until the Soviet Union fell in 1991. The alliances avoided direct war—no one wanted World War

III! Yet, the rivalry and competition led to international incidents that almost plunged the world into nuclear war.

Churchill (UK), Truman (US), and Stalin (USSR) at the end of WWII[17]

The two sides were incredibly suspicious and resentful of each other, often with good reason. Both sides used sly tactics to convince other countries in Africa, Asia, Central America, and South America to align with them. They offered economic benefits and showered them with propaganda. **Propaganda** is information (often disinformation) used to convince people that one side is right and the other is wrong. **Disinformation** is false information intentionally spread to deceive people.

What Was the Arms Race?

America's policy during the Cold War was *containment*—preventing the Soviet Union from expanding any further. To this end, the United States built up its weapons like never before. America had already shown the world what it could do when it dropped two atomic bombs on Japan. It increased defense spending exponentially, developing and increasing nuclear weapons.

Of course, the Soviet Union had to keep up. It had already started developing an atomic bomb during World War II. The Soviets correctly suspected Britain, America, and Germany were doing the same. At the end of the war, the Soviets captured the German nuclear scientists and used them to surge ahead in making their own bomb.

The Soviets desperately needed uranium for their bomb project. The Americans had grabbed up most of Germany's uranium ore stash as

WWII ended. However, the Soviets found a hundred metric tons of uranium oxide (the refined product made from uranium ore) in Austria and another hundred tons in Germany. In 1949, the Soviet Union tested its atom bomb, "First Lightning," in Kazakhstan.

President Truman responded, "I have directed the Atomic Energy Commission to continue its work on all forms of atomic weapons, including the so-called hydrogen or superbomb."[i]

The race was on for the superbomb! What is the difference between an atom bomb and a ***hydrogen bomb***? Atomic bombs use split atoms (***nuclear fission***) to cause the explosion. Hydrogen (thermonuclear) bombs use both split atoms and fused atoms. A hydrogen bomb detonates when a small atom bomb triggers the reaction that fuses atoms (***nuclear fusion***). Hydrogen bombs are a thousand times more powerful than atom bombs.

In the 1950s and 1960s, Americans lived in terror of nuclear bombs. They dug bomb shelters in their backyards. The Federal Civil Defense Administration ordered schools to put children through "duck and cover" drills. Students watched training films featuring "Bert the Turtle." They practiced diving under their desks so they would know what to do if a bomb dropped.

A 1962 school "duck and cover" drill[ii]

---

[i] "Statement by the President on the Hydrogen Bomb," The American Presidency Project, Accessed January 4, 2025, https://www.presidency.ucsb.edu/documents/statement-the-president-the-hydrogen-bomb.

Would hiding under a desk have worked if an actual nuclear bomb hit? A bomb's shockwave and intense heat would immediately kill anything within about a mile. Flying debris would extend several miles, so the desks would have helped protect against shattering glass and falling objects. However, lethal radiation would travel up to a hundred miles, depending on the wind.

What Was the Cuban Missile Crisis? (1962)

The United States's relationship with Cuba, only ninety miles south of Key West, was complicated. Cuba had been independent since 1902, and the two countries initially enjoyed a close friendship. Americans, especially the rich and famous, flocked to Cuba to enjoy its beaches, palm trees, casinos, and vibrant nightlife. Then, Fidel Castro led a revolution against Cuba's brutal dictator Fulgencio Batista. In 1959, Batista fled Cuba, and Castro took power.

The United States recognized Castro's government immediately. However, the friendship fell apart when Castro formed a Communist government and established close ties with the Soviet Union. The CIA under President Kennedy launched the failed Bay of Pigs invasion in 1961. The CIA had trained 1,400 Cubans who had fled to America. In part one of the plan, the exiles were supposed to take out Cuba's air force. However, Castro discovered the plot and moved his aircraft in time.

The next part of the plan was to invade the Bay of Pigs on Cuba's southern shore. Despite the CIA's attempts to keep the raid a secret, word got out to the Cubans once again. What's worse, some of the exiles' ships hit reefs and sank, and their paratroopers landed in the wrong place. Castro's troops killed 114 exiles and captured most of the rest. Many people expected President Kennedy to send American troops in at this point. However, he refused. He did not want to spark the Soviets' wrath and start World War III.

The Cuban Missile Crisis erupted the following year. In this stressful, thirteen-day standoff between America and the Soviet Union, the Cold War suddenly got hot. The Soviets installed nuclear-armed SS-4 medium-range ballistic missiles in Cuba. The rockets were within easy striking range of Florida and other targets in the eastern United States. For the Soviets, it was payback for all the missiles America had aimed at them from Turkey and Western Europe.

In October 1962, an American pilot flying a spy plane high over Cuba spotted and photographed a missile. When President Kennedy got word, his executive committee wrestled with what to do. How could they get rid of the missiles without triggering nuclear war? They discussed invading Cuba or bombing the rockets. However, Kennedy's final decision was to place a blockade of Navy ships around Cuba to prevent the Soviets from sending more missiles. Next, he gave the Soviet Union an ultimatum: remove the missiles or face American military wrath.

Kennedy hashes out a plan with his generals.[30]

Kennedy made a television broadcast on October 22, 1962, telling the American public about the missiles and what he was doing about it. Americans were on pins and needles. Some hoarded food and gasoline, certain they were on the brink of war. Two days later, Soviet ships approached the US Navy blockade around Cuba. Yet, they stopped. They did not try to get through.

Kennedy and his advisors breathed a sigh of relief. However, those missiles were still there in Cuba. Three days later, the Cubans shot down an American spy plane flying over Cuba. Tensions ran high. Kennedy's team had been exchanging communication with the Soviet leadership. Finally, Nikita Khrushchev, premier of the Soviet Union, blinked. On October 26, he messaged Kennedy. "I'll remove the missiles if you promise not to invade Cuba." The next day, he sent additional terms: "Also, remove your missiles in Turkey."

Kennedy exhaled. He officially announced America would not invade Cuba. He pretended to ignore the part about the missiles in Turkey. Nevertheless, he quietly removed them. The Cuban Missile Crisis ended on October 28. The following year, the Americans and Soviets established a "hotline" between Washington D.C. and Moscow. They signed treaties regarding nuclear weapons. However, it was not the end of the Cold War. The Soviets shifted their focus to developing ballistic missiles that could reach the US from the Soviet Union.

Who Won the Space Race?

In the Cold War, the United States and the Soviet Union competed for a commanding influence on planet Earth, but they did not stop there. They also competed for space. America's history has always been one of exploration and expansion. Space became the final frontier—and yet the Soviets got into space first.

On October 4, 1957, the Soviet Union launched *Sputnik I* (Russian for "traveler"). It was the first manmade satellite to leave Earth's atmosphere. The Soviets used an R-7 intercontinental ballistic missile to thrust it 139 miles from Earth. It circled Earth 1,440 times for the next three months. Finally, aerodynamic drag pulled it out of orbit and back into Earth's atmosphere. The denser air levels caused friction and intense heat, and the satellite burst into flames and burned up. The Space Race involved not only getting an object into space but bringing it back safely.

One month later, the Soviet Union launched a second satellite, *Sputnik 2*. This satellite had a living passenger: a mixed-breed dog named Laika. She had been a stray on Moscow's streets. Laika died from overheating about five hours after the satellite launched. The insulation came loose, and the satellite's nose cone did not drop off as it should have. That caused the thermal system to malfunction, and the temperature rose to 104 Fahrenheit, too hot for a dog to survive for long. *Sputnik 2* orbited Earth for five months and then burned up when it reentered Earth's atmosphere as *Sputnik 1* had done.

Laika, the first animal in space[40]

The news about the two satellites stunned America. It was embarrassing that the Soviets got into space first. Yet, there were more insidious implications. The technology that got the satellites out there could easily deliver a nuclear warhead into the United States. America's rocket scientists were already making progress on their own space technology, and they ramped things up. It was time to show the Soviets what they could do.

President Eisenhower created NASA, the National Aeronautics and Space Administration, in 1958. On February 1, three months after *Sputnik 2* was launched, the Americans launched their first satellite, *Explorer 1*, from Cape Canaveral, Florida. *Explorer 1* circled Earth for twelve years and burned up when it reentered the atmosphere in 1970. In 1959, the Soviets sent the first (unmanned) spacecraft to the moon. It hit the moon at 7,400 miles per hour.

On April 12, 1961, the Soviets sent the first man, Yuri Alekseyevich Gagarin, into space. He orbited Earth one time. It took 108 minutes. Fortunately for Yuri, the Soviet rocket scientists had figured out how to get a rocket back into the atmosphere without bursting into flames. It did go into a spin as it entered, but Yuri managed to stay conscious. Four miles above Earth, the spacecraft ejected Yuri. His parachute opened at 8,200 feet, and he floated safely to the ground. Another parachute brought the spaceship to a gentle landing.

American Alan Shepard flew into space three weeks after Yuri Gagarin. Then, the Americans finally outdid the Soviets when they flew Neil Armstrong and Buzz Aldrin to the moon in July 1969. Armstrong was the first man to stand on the moon, saying, "One small step for man, one giant leap for mankind." Aldrin joined him on the moon's surface, and they spent over two hours exploring and collecting material to bring back to Earth.

Buzz Aldrin on the moon, 1969. Photo by Neil A. Armstrong.[41]

Who won the Space Race? Although the Soviets got a head start, America ultimately won. The Soviets never put a man on the moon. From 1968 to 1971, twelve American men walked on the moon.

Who won the Cold War? America did when the Soviet Union collapsed in 1991.

In recent years, a silly conspiracy theory has surfaced, arguing that walking on the moon was all a hoax. The theory is easily debunked. The astronauts videoed themselves on the moon. Millions of Americans were glued to their television sets, watching the men leap about on the moon, which has lower gravity than Earth. The astronauts took thousands of photos. They left footprints behind, which the Lunar Reconnaissance Orbiter (LRO) photographed in 2009. They also brought moon rocks and moon dust home to be tested.

Roundup Activity: Two Truths and a Lie

Spot which one of the three statements in each grouping is a lie. Check your answers in the back of the book.

- The USSR covered one-sixth of the planet at its peak.
- The USSR achieved superpower status before World War I.
- The USSR's political ideology was at odds with American democratic ideals.
- NATO was an alliance of the US, Canada, and European countries to defend themselves against a potential attack from a "third party" (primarily the Soviet Union).
- NATO and the Warsaw Pact alliances set off the Cold War.
- The Cold War ended in 1962 after the Cuban Missile Crisis was resolved.
- Atom bombs are much more powerful than hydrogen bombs.
- The Soviets used captured German nuclear scientists to develop an atom bomb.
- American schoolchildren had drills where they practiced hiding under the desk for protection from nuclear bombs.
- The USSR installed nuclear-armed ballistic missiles in Cuba, only ninety miles from Florida.
- President Kennedy put a navy blockade around Cuba.
- The Soviet missiles never got removed from Cuba.
- America sent the first man-made satellite into space.
- A dog named Laika was the first animal in space.
- America won the Space Race by putting men on the moon.

Chapter 8: The War on Terror

On September 11, 2001, the deadliest foreign attack on American soil ignited the War on Terror. That morning, nineteen Islamic al Qaeda (*el Kai duh*) terrorists hijacked four American passenger jets.

At 7:59 a.m., American Airlines Flight 11 left Logan International Airport in Boston, heading to Los Angeles. A few minutes into the flight, five terrorists attacked the crew and forced their way into the cockpit. They diverted the plane toward New York City in a suicide attack.

A flight attendant, Betty Ong, managed to call the reservations center in North Carolina. "The cockpit is not answering their phone. We can't get in. The door won't open. Our number one has been stabbed, our number five has been stabbed. And our purser had been stabbed." (Numbers one and five were flight attendants.)

Betty wasn't scheduled to be on the flight but had joined it to get to Los Angeles to meet her sister. They were planning a vacation in Hawaii. Unnoticed in the back of the plane, she stayed on the phone for twenty-six minutes. Her last words were, "Pray for us. Pray for us."

And then, eerie silence. "Betty? Betty? Are you still there?"

At 8:46 a.m., American Airlines Flight 11 flew into the North Tower of the World Trade Center, between floors 95 and 99. All ninety-two people on the airplane died. Seventeen minutes later, United Airlines Flight 175 crashed into the World Trade Center's South Tower, between floors 77 and 85. It killed the sixty-six people on board. The two crashes killed 2,606 people in the World Trade Center or on the ground, including 441 firefighters and other first responders trying to rescue the victims.

September 11, 2001, attack on the World Trade Center⁴⁸

As New York City erupted into confusion, more drama unfolded in the sky. Terrorists had already hijacked American Airlines Flight 77 on its way from Dulles International Airport in Virginia to Los Angeles. A passenger, Barbara Colson, and a flight attendant, Renee May, called their loved ones. Renee was pregnant with her first child. The hijackers turned Flight 77 around and headed east. At 9:37 a.m., the terrorists crashed into the Pentagon, killing everyone in the plane and 153 military and defense employees in the building.

United Airlines Flight 93 left Newark International Airport in New Jersey at 8:42 a.m., headed for San Francisco. It was behind schedule and only in the air for four minutes before the first plane flew into the World Trade Center. Air traffic control sent a warning to Flight 93 at 9:23 a.m. Confused, the pilot responded, "Confirm latest message, please." Two minutes later, the terrorists broke into the cockpit. The pilot screamed, "Mayday! Mayday!" as the plane dropped 685 feet.

By this point, the passengers were calling family members and officials on the ground. One passenger, Ted Burnett, called his wife several times. He told her the terrorists had stabbed a passenger and claimed to have a bomb. His wife told him about the attacks on the World Trade Center. Ted realized the terrorists were plotting the same thing with his plane. "Oh my God! It's a suicide mission!"

Ted and three other passengers—Mark Bingham, Todd Beamer, and Jeremy Glick—planned to retake the plane from the hijackers. The airplane was descending, and they knew it was targeting something. "We're going to rush the hijackers," Glick told his wife. They planned to fly the airplane into the ground before it could hit the intended target. Beamer recited the Lord's Prayer and Psalm 23: "Yea, though I walk through the valley of the shadow of death, I will fear no evil, for thou art with me."

They stormed the cockpit. In the ensuing struggle, the airplane crashed into a field in Pennsylvania. The suspected target was the White House. President George W. Bush wasn't there. That morning, he was reading books to the children at Emma E. Booker Elementary School in Sarasota, Florida. The White House Chief of Staff whispered in his ear about the two attacks on the World Trade Center. Bush quietly got up to take a phone call from Condoleezza Rice, the national security director. After hanging up, Bush told his staff, "We're at war."

President Bush meets with his Security Council on September 12, 2001[48]

The war was not against a specific country. It was a war on terror. President Bush addressed the nation:

"The attack took place on American soil, but it was an attack on the heart and soul of the civilized world. And the world has come together to fight a new and different war, the first, and we hope the only one, of the twenty-first century. A war against all those who seek to export terror, and a war against those governments that support or shelter them."[i]

Who Was Osama bin Laden?

Osama bin Laden was the mastermind behind the September 11 hijackings. He was the son of a billionaire in Saudi Arabia's construction business, and his father was a close friend of the Saudi royal family. Interestingly, bin Laden had fifty-two brothers and sisters from his father's twenty-two wives. Muslims are only supposed to have four wives (at a time). His father stayed married to three of his wives but constantly changed out the fourth wife. Bin Laden's mother was from Syria and the last wife his father married.

Osama bin Laden attended King Abdul Aziz University, where he embraced an extreme, radical form of Islam. The Soviet Union invaded Afghanistan in 1979 when bin Laden was twenty-two. Since Afghanistan was primarily Muslim, bin Laden considered this an attack on Islam. He spearheaded a resistance movement using his family's money. In 1988, he created *al-Qaeda*, a network of militants recruited from around the Muslim world.

What Did the Taliban and Al-Qaeda Have in Common?

The Soviets withdrew from Afghanistan in 1989, and bin Laden made it his headquarters in 1996. By this point, the *Taliban* had taken over most of Afghanistan, and it welcomed bin Laden. The Taliban is a political and religious organization that follows strict Islamic law. Taliban rule was brutal and repressive, especially toward women. Even today, girls cannot attend school after sixth grade, and only a handful of jobs are available for women.

---

[i] George W. Bush, "Global War on Terror," George W. Bush Presidential Library, Accessed January 4, 2025, https://www.georgewbushlibrary.gov/research/topic-guides/global-war-terror.

Al-Qaeda and the Taliban shared similar objectives and ideology. However, al-Qaeda's plans were global. The organization planned to create a *caliphate*, a political-religious state, led by a man following Islamic law. Al-Qaeda considered the United States its biggest enemy.

The Taliban's goals were modest and localized compared to Al-Qaeda. The Taliban wanted to subdue corrupt warlords in Afghanistan and establish a government with *Sharia law* based on the Quran (the Muslim holy book) and the opinions of Muslim teachers.

Bin Laden (l) and his advisor, Ayman al-Zawahiri in 2001"

Some examples of the Taliban's interpretation of Sharia law include banning women from many public areas. Women must have a male guardian with them and keep their hair and face covered whenever they step outside their homes. Sharia law says that if a Muslim leaves the Islamic faith, he must be killed. Al-Qaeda also followed Sharia law, but its members were slightly less strict with women and girls.

What Were Al-Qaeda's Goals in the September 11 Attacks?

Bin Laden believed the United States was already in a weakened state. For instance, America withdrew its troops from Lebanon after terrorists bombed the US Marine barracks in 1983. America withdrew from

Somalia in 1993. Osama bin Laden wanted to further weaken the United States' standing in the world. More than anything, he wanted fear to reign—in America and worldwide. He hoped that the United States would stop supporting Middle Eastern governments that did not follow strict Sharia law.

President Bush's Response to the September 11 Attacks

On September 20, President Bush initiated the "GWOT" or "Global War on Terror" to find and stop terrorists worldwide. America partnered with other like-minded countries. Initially, the focus was on Afghanistan and then Iraq. However, it also used diplomatic and financial incentives to discourage other countries from harboring terrorists. "Our war on terror begins with al Qaeda, but it does not end there. It will not end until every terrorist group of global reach has been found, stopped, and defeated," Bush stated.

On October 7, 2001, Bush announced military strikes had begun against al-Qaeda and the Taliban in Afghanistan:

> "As we strike military targets, we'll also drop food, medicine, and supplies to the starving and suffering men and women and children of Afghanistan. The United States of America is a friend to the Afghan people, and we are the friends of almost a billion worldwide who practice the Islamic faith."

How Did Iraq Get Involved?

Iraq's president, Saddam Hussein, was a threat to peace in the Middle East. However, the CIA found no proof of a connection with bin Laden. Hussein hated the United States, which had led a coalition to fight against him successfully in the 1990-91 Gulf War. Hussein started the Gulf War by invading Kuwait and had started an earlier war by invading Iran in 1980. The Middle Eastern nations considered him a loose cannon, constantly stirring up trouble.

Fighter jets from the US, Canada, Qatar, and France fly over Saudi Arabia in the Gulf War.⁴⁵

Hussein had committed horrible human rights violations, such as using mustard gas and Sarin nerve gas against Kurdish men, women, and children. He wiped out thousands of villages. President Bush reported Hussein was developing weapons of mass destruction, like anthrax and nuclear weapons. Hussein never developed an atomic bomb, but he did build a nuclear reactor. The only thing that stopped him from building a nuclear bomb was the lack of fissile material.

On March 19, 2003, the United States invaded Iraq to remove Hussein as Iraq's president. The country fell almost immediately, but Hussein disappeared. Finally, in December, American soldiers found him hiding in a hole in the ground. In June 2004, the US handed him over to the interim Iraqi government. It charged him with crimes against humanity, including torturing women and children and murdering 148 Shiite people. (The Shiites followed a different form of Islam.) The court found him guilty, and he died by hanging in December 2006.

The War on Terror Redefined

The War on Terror began as a coalition between the United States, the United Kingdom, and other allies. Their target was terrorists, specifically those in the Middle East. When Barack Obama became president in 2009, his goal in the Middle East was to get rid of al-Qaeda. Killing or capturing bin Laden was his top priority. When al-Qaeda was eliminated, the war would be over. It was no longer the "Global War on Terror." Now, it was part of "Overseas Contingency Operations." Journalists groaned. How could they sell headlines with a name like that?

Operation Neptune Spear: Navy Seals Take Out Osama bin Laden

When American troops moved into Afghanistan in 2001, bin Laden slipped into hiding. A decade passed, and US intelligence was unsure of his location. Intelligence officials did, however, gather several clues over the years. They knew he wasn't using phones anymore—they were too easy to track. They discovered he had been communicating with al-Qaeda through a trusted courier named al-Kuwaiti. Yet, where was al-Kuwaiti? Could he be on the run with bin Laden?

In 2007, US intelligence got more information on al-Kuwaiti. His real name was Ahmed, and he was from Pakistan. They heard a rumor that bin Laden was staying in Ahmed's family compound in Pakistan. They found Ahmed (al-Kuwaiti) in August 2010 and secretly followed him to his compound. Could bin Laden be in there?

The CIA studied surveillance photos of the compound. It appeared to be custom-built to hide someone. It was at the end of a dead-end road outside the city, surrounded by a twelve-foot concrete wall topped with barbed wire. The home had no internet or telephone service (making it hard to tap). While the neighbors set their trash out to be picked up by the garbage truck, the people in this home burned their trash. The CIA made the educated guess that bin Laden was there with his youngest wife and children.

On May 1, 2011, at 10:30 p.m., two helicopters carried twenty-three Navy SEALs from Team Six into Pakistan from Afghanistan. Typically, SEALs rappel down from a hovering helicopter; however, one of the helicopters destabilized and had to land inside the compound. As they approached a guesthouse wearing night vision goggles, someone shot at them through the door. They returned fire. Several minutes later, a woman opened the door with a baby on her hip and more children behind her. The SEALs went inside and found al-Kuwaiti (Ahmed) lying dead.

As they entered the main house, bin Laden's adult son, Khalid, shot at them from the second floor. They returned fire and killed him. The

SEALs continued up to the third floor as bullets flew. They found Osama bin Laden in a bedroom with two of his wives. One wife rushed at the SEALs, blocking bin Laden and getting shot in the leg. A two-year-old boy wailed in the corner. Two SEALs threw themselves on the women to protect them. Bin Laden exchanged fire with the SEALs, and two bullets pierced his head. The mastermind of the September 11, 2001, attack that killed nearly three thousand people on American soil was dead.

A newspaper announcement of bin Laden's death [46]

Roundup Activity: Multiple Choice Quiz (first eight chapters)

1. How did the first Americans get to America?
   a. They crossed the Beringia land bridge.
   b. They crossed the Atlantic Ocean from Europe.
   c. They always lived there.
   d. They migrated from South America.

2. What did the Indigenous Americans teach the European colonists?
   a. How to farm with the Three Sisters planting system
   b. How to grow and use tobacco
   c. Both a and b
   d. None of the above

3. Who believed that all children—boys and girls—should be educated?
   a. The Catholics in Maryland
   b. The Puritans in New England
   c. The Spanish colonists in Florida
   d. The Virginia Colony

4. Who wrote the Declaration of Independence?
   a. Benjamin Franklin
   b. George Washington
   c. Paul Revere
   d. Thomas Jefferson

5. Which political party was pro-slavery when it first began?
   a. Democrat
   b. Libertarian
   c. Republican
   d. Socialist

6. Whose submarine sunk the USS *Housatonic*?
    a. The Confederates
    b. The Union
    c. The Canadians
    d. None of the above

7. Why did Mrs. Rosa Parks get arrested?
    a. She refused to move to the back of the bus.
    b. She helped organize a bus boycott.
    c. Both a and b
    d. None of the above

8. What was different about World War I?
    a. Tanks were used for the first time.
    b. Machine guns became a key weapon.
    c. The female employment rate doubled.
    d. All of the above

9. Who masterminded the September 11, 2001, attacks on the United States?
    a. King Abdul Aziz
    b. Osama bin Laden
    c. Saddam Hussein
    d. All of the above

10. How did the CIA figure out bin Laden was in the compound in Pakistan?
    a. They followed his associate Ahmed (al-Kuwaiti).
    b. The home had no internet or phone service.
    c. The people in the home burned their trash rather than using the garbage pickup.
    d. All of the above

Chapter 9: Presidential Progress

Who were the best presidents? Who were the worst? That, of course, is a matter of opinion. How do historians judge the best and worst? They consider their moral authority, international relations, vision, and how they handled crises. How well did they relate with Congress and handle the economy during their presidencies? Even the "best" presidents had severe flaws, yet they contributed positively to America's history.

This chapter reviews the seven best presidents, according to multiple historians, and what made them stand out. It also reviews the three worst presidents in American history. No one who has served in the past twenty-five years is on the list. Time needs to pass to assess a president's lasting impact. The presidents are listed in order of when they were president. However, most historians agree that George Washington, Abraham Lincoln, and Franklin Roosevelt were the top three.

Who Were the Seven Best Presidents?

George Washington (1789–97)

Washington was a war hero who led the colonists in winning independence. He also worked with other patriots to set up the United States government. He was the natural choice for America's first president and served for two four-year terms.

America was war-torn and almost bankrupt when Washington became president. He kept America from further wars by not getting involved in European conflicts. Washington paid each state's war debt from the federal treasury. He put a 5 percent tax on all imports so the treasury could pay the debt. The countries that imported goods were paying the debt, not the Americans.

George Washington in a 1796 painting by Gilbert Stuart [47]

Washington warned Americans not to have political parties but to work as a unit. "Parties will divide Americans!" Washington established the United States Mint, which made coins. He made the dollar America's official currency. Dollars were silver coins then; the US did not use paper money until 1861.

Thomas Jefferson (1801–09)

Jefferson was America's third president. In 1796, he lost to John Adams by three electoral votes. Jefferson became Adam's vice president due to a glitch in the Constitution. He barely won the next election. Jefferson cut military spending, reduced the budget, and decreased the national debt by one-third. In 1803, he bought the Louisiana Territory from France. It was a bit of a gamble because the Constitution did not permit the government to buy foreign territory. To his relief, the Senate voted 24-7 to approve the purchase.

Thomas Jefferson, 1805 portrait by Rembrandt Peale[48]

Jefferson spent his second term trying to keep America out of Napoleon's wars in Europe. The British were boarding American ships and forcing thousands of American sailors into their navy to fight Napoleon. When three American sailors escaped the British Navy, Britain brazenly demanded them back. A British ship even fired on an American ship, killing three men. Jefferson passed the ***Non-Intercourse Act of 1809*** to end the nonsense. It stopped British imports and banned British ships from American waters.

Abraham Lincoln (1861–65)

Abraham Lincoln grew up in poverty on the Kentucky and Indiana frontier, coming of age during the Second Great Awakening. His mother died when he was nine, and he did not go to school much because he had to help his father on the farm. However, Lincoln learned to read, which became his favorite pastime. He borrowed books on history, law, and other themes and self-educated himself. His life exemplifies how anyone can succeed through dedication and determination.

Did you know that Lincoln only had a beard for the last four years of his life? When he was running for president, an eleven-year-old girl named Grace encouraged him to grow a beard to get more votes. He did, and he got elected!

Abraham Lincoln in 1860, just before growing a beard[49]

As we learned earlier, Lincoln was the president during the Civil War, which almost ripped the United States apart. He did everything within his power to preserve the Union. Lincoln had to make many difficult choices. It was impossible to please everyone. Nevertheless, he guided the nation through the crisis.

Lincoln was murdered just as the war ended, but he promoted reconciliation for the rebellious states rather than punishment. Just weeks before, at his Second Inaugural Address, he urged, "Let us strive to finish the work we are in; to bind up the nation's wounds … to do all which may achieve and cherish a just, and a lasting peace."

Theodore Roosevelt (1901–09)

In 1901, an assassin shot President McKinley. Suddenly, Vice-President "Teddy" Roosevelt was America's new leader. He was the cowboy president. Before his political career took off, he went to North Dakota to hunt buffalo, fell in love with the plains, and bought a cattle ranch. Roosevelt was a "Rough Rider" (volunteer cavalry) during the Spanish-American War. President Roosevelt loved the great outdoors and gave federal protection to wildlife and land. He created 5 national parks, 51 bird reserves, and 150 national forests. He placed over 230 million acres under government protection.

Colonel Roosevelt, the Rough Rider, three years before becoming president[50]

Roosevelt had the Panama Canal built through a fifty-mile stretch of Panama so ships could pass from the Caribbean Sea to the Pacific Ocean (or vice versa). Before the canal, ships traveling between America's eastern shores and Asia had to sail around the bottom of South America, a long and dangerous voyage.

Roosevelt broke up giant business monopolies, like the ones controlling America's railroad lines. He used antitrust laws that promoted competition and fair trade to do this. In 1902, the coal miners in Pennsylvania went on strike. Winter was setting in, and people needed coal to heat their homes. Roosevelt called the mine owners and the miners to the White House, but the owners refused to negotiate. "Okay, then," Roosevelt replied with a glint in his eye. "I'll have my military seize the mines. I'll run them as a federal operation."

Suddenly, the mine owners were ready to negotiate. Roosevelt called it his "Square Deal" because everyone benefitted fairly. Roosevelt used a similar approach when dealing with other countries. He loved to say, "Speak softly and carry a big stick."

Franklin D. Roosevelt (1933–45)

Americans loved Franklin Roosevelt so much that they elected him to four terms. (In 1951, the US limited presidents to two terms.) Known as FDR, he was a distant cousin of Teddy Roosevelt. FDR became president in the fourth year of the Great Depression (1929-39). Twenty-five percent of America's workforce had lost their jobs. Could he pull the United States out of its economic slump?

Roosevelt's Emergency Banking Act let the Federal Reserve insure bank deposits. Even if a bank failed, people who had deposited money into the bank could get their money. His economic plans helped a little, but pulling out of the slump took years. FDR introduced Social Security for seniors and assistance for disabled people. He made "oppressive child labor" illegal and gave America the forty-hour work week and minimum wage.

FDR (center) with Churchill and Stalin at the Yalta Summit two months before he died[51]

As discussed earlier, Roosevelt successfully guided the United States through WWII. His health went downhill quickly in his fourth term, which his staff kept a secret. He died while in office on April 12, 1945. Mussolini's execution and Hitler's suicide were just days later. The war in Europe ended three weeks after Roosevelt's death.

John F. Kennedy (1961–63)

John F. Kennedy served less than three years before two assassin's bullets ended his life. Yet, he left a lasting legacy. In 1963, he signed the Limited Test Ban Treaty with the Soviet Union and the United Kingdom. It banned nuclear weapons testing above ground to prevent poisoning the air and water with radiation. Kennedy established the *Peace Corps*, a government program that sends trained volunteers to help developing countries. He picked up Dwight Eisenhower's *Apollo Program* and set the goal of putting a man on the moon.

John F. Kennedy and his nephew, Robert F. Kennedy Jr., with a pet salamander[58]

In his 1963 speech on civil rights, Kennedy asked, "If an American, because his skin is dark, cannot eat lunch in a restaurant open to the public, if he cannot send his children to the best public school available, if he cannot vote for the public officials who represent him, if, in short, he cannot enjoy the full and free life which all of us want, then who among us would be content to have the color of his skin changed and stand in his place?"

Kennedy made outstanding progress in integrating America's public schools and universities before his murder. Eight months after his death, the Civil Rights Act of 1964 passed. It banned discrimination based on race, religion, gender, or national origin and established equal employment.

Ronald Reagan (1981–89)

Ronald Reagan was the movie star who became president. After serving in WWII, he became a political activist, speaking out against racism and the Ku Klux Klan. Reagan became California's governor in 1966 and president in 1981, serving two terms. He was struck by a would-be assassin's bullet two months after becoming president. It punctured his lung and caused massive internal bleeding that put him in the hospital for six weeks.

Reagan meets with Prince Charles (now King Charles III of the United Kingdom).[58]

America enjoyed eight years of peace during Reagan's two terms. He appointed the first woman, Sandra Day O'Connor, to the Supreme Court. He also negotiated an arms reduction accord with the Soviet Union. Reagan worked closely with Soviet ruler Mikhail Gorbachev as he restructured the USSR from communism to a social democracy.

Reagan communicated his policies and goals in simple language that everyone could understand. He boosted the morale of the American people, who had become pessimistic and worried. He commented, "What I'd really like to do is go down in history as the President who made Americans believe in themselves again." Reagan achieved that goal.

His economic policy, nicknamed "Reaganomics," involved tax cuts that helped jumpstart the stagnating economy. He also tried to reduce government regulations over business. Unemployment dropped as twenty-one million new jobs opened. Inflation plunged, and production rose. However, critics pointed out that the rich got richer while more people became poor.

Who Were the Three Worst Presidents?

Interestingly, the three men most historians say were the worst presidents all served within twelve years of each other. This was in the era just before and immediately after the Civil War. It was an agonizing time for America.

Franklin Pierce (1853–57)

Franklin Pierce, portrait by Mathew Brady[4]

When the Democrats tried to nominate a presidential candidate in 1852, they sharply disagreed over the three top contenders. That's when Pierce came to mind. He was relatively unknown and did not have strong opinions on anything. People would not be able to find fault with him. He was the vanilla candidate. Pierce did not even campaign against his opponent, "Old Fuss and Feathers" Winfield Scott. People disliked Scott so much that Pierce won by a landslide.

Pierce became president a few years before the Civil War. Americans were hotly divided on the slavery issue. Although Pierce was from New Hampshire, he opposed freeing enslaved people. He approved of returning escaped slaves to their owners in the South. In 1854, Pierce signed the Kansas-Nebraska Act that canceled a ban on slavery in the Northern territories. This act divided America even more intensely, leading to a political firestorm between the pro-slavers and the abolitionists. Pierce's attempts to stop the violent demonstrations were inept.

James Buchanan (1857–61)

Buchanan came after Pierce and inherited his mess. He felt the voters in the new territories should decide what to do about slavery. Of course, the voters were all White men. He also supported the Supreme Court decision that Dred Scott was not a citizen despite living his entire life in the United States.

In 1859, an anti-slavery activist named John Brown led an attack on a federal arsenal in Harper's Ferry near Washington, D.C. He wanted weapons for his struggle against slavery. Brown captured the armory and set the local enslaved people free. However, the following morning, the Marines stormed the arsenal and arrested Brown and several accomplices. Brown was hanged six weeks later with President Buchanan's approval. Tensions soared, and the divide between the North and South deepened, exploding into war two years later.

James Buchanan by Matthew Brady[65]

Andrew Johnson (1865–69)

Andrew Johnson became president when Abraham Lincoln was shot. Despite being Lincoln's vice president, Johnson had owned several enslaved people. He freed them in 1853 and kept them as paid servants. After unexpectedly becoming president, Johnson sparred with his advisors on what post-war America should look like. Would Black people have voting rights? What did the rebel states need to do to be readmitted into the Union?

President Johnson vetoed bills promoting equality and civil rights. He assured Missouri's governor, "This is a country for White men, and by God, as long as I am President, it shall be a government for White men." He was against the Fourteenth Amendment, which gave citizenship to formerly enslaved people. This led to a two-year battle between the president and the Republican Party, the bill's champions. In 1866, the Republicans took Congress by a landslide and pushed the bill through a year later.

Andrew Johnson, photographed by Mathew Benjamin Brady[66]

The Congress also tried to pass the *Civil Rights Act*, which gave formerly enslaved people full citizenship and said they had the same rights as Whites regarding property ownership and contracts. Similar wording was in the Fourteenth Amendment, but that had not passed yet. President Johnson vetoed the Civil Rights Act. Congress passed the bill again, and Johnson vetoed it again. This time, however, the Republicans and other bill supporters had a two-thirds majority in the House and Senate and overrode Johnson's veto.

In 1868, Johnson fired his secretary of war, Edwin Stanton, without getting the Senate's go-ahead. Stanton was a Republican hired by Abraham Lincoln. The "Radical Republicans" impeached Johnson in February 1868 for breaking the Tenure of Office Act. However, seven senators voted against the impeachment, and Johnson survived as president. The seven senators were not fans of Johnson. The issue was that Johnson did not have a vice president. If they impeached him, the Senate president, Benjamin Wade, would become president. The senators thought he would be worse than Johnson.

Roundup Activity: Election Poster

Choose one of the above presidents and pretend you are part of his election campaign. Create an election poster with key facts you think would be essential to voters.

Chapter 10: Star-Spangled Heroes and Villains

The people in this chapter were not presidents or famous politicians. Most came from humble backgrounds. They rose to fame through other ways, like athletics, activism, and inventions. Some were heroes, and some were villains. Some were both. Yet, they all played a key role in shaping American history.

Benedict Arnold

Benedict Arnold was an American war hero who turned traitor. He was born in 1741 in Connecticut. His father was an alcoholic, and when he lost his business, Benedict had to leave school at age fourteen. His dreams of going to Yale crumbled. At sixteen, Benedict briefly served in the French and Indian War. He then opened a small store in New Haven, Connecticut, and soon became a wealthy businessman.

As a captain in the American Revolutionary War, Arnold successfully captured the British Fort Ticonderoga and Fort George in New York in 1775. However, he got passed over for promotion.

Arnold launched a successful defense when the British attacked a supply depot in Connecticut. A bullet shattered his left leg, and another bullet killed his horse, and it fell on his right leg. As blood gushed from Arnold's leg, his men finally got the dead horse off him. Due to the chaos of war, they could not get him to a hospital until four days later. Gangrene had set in, and antibiotics had not yet been discovered. The surgeon recommended amputating the leg. "I'd rather die," Arnold answered. All the doctors could do was clean and drain the wound. After months in the hospital in agonizing pain, he survived with a leg two inches shorter than the other. Despite all this, his political enemies gave a medal to another officer for the battle. However, George Washington intervened, and Congress promoted Arnold to major general.

Benedict Arnold in 1776, painted by Thomas Hart[67]

Arnold's enemies weren't done. Arnold was court-martialed and received a humiliating public reprimand in 1781 for a minor offense. Enough was enough! He began negotiating with the British about switching sides. Meanwhile, the unsuspecting American military put him in charge of West Point. Arnold secretly worked to weaken the fort's defenses.

The British rewarded him financially and made him brigadier general for coming over to their side. Arnold led two British attacks in 1781. In Virginia, he captured Richmond, and in Connecticut, he burned New London to the ground. He and his wife then sailed to Britain, where he died twenty years later.

Susan B. Anthony

Susan B. Anthony was an American hero who fought to end slavery and give women the right to vote. She was born in 1820 in Massachusetts to a Quaker family who taught the equality of all people before God. In 1845, Anthony's family moved to Rochester, New York, and their home became a central meeting place for the anti-slavery movement. She began traveling around, giving lectures against slavery. She even challenged Abraham Lincoln for being too moderate on the issue.

Anthony got a job as a teacher in 1848. She discovered male teachers made four times the salary of female teachers. She began fighting for women's equal rights, including ***women's suffrage,*** or the right to vote. Anthony met Elizabeth Cady Stanton, who organized the first women's rights convention. The ladies became lifelong friends as they pioneered women's rights and fought to end slavery.

Susan B. Anthony, engraved by G.E. Perine & Co.[38]

In 1863, Anthony formed the Women's Loyal National League with Stanton and Lucy Stone. They fought for an amendment to the Constitution to end slavery. Two years later, their dream came true when the Thirteenth Amendment abolished slavery. However, Anthony was disappointed when the Fifteenth Amendment passed. Black men could finally vote, but no women could vote.

In January 1869, Anthony held the first women's suffrage conference in Washington, D.C. She told women to go out and register to vote, even though it wasn't legal. In 1872, she and a group of ladies walked to a local barber shop, a place to register to vote in those days. The registrar was so surprised that he let them register. On Election Day, Anthony cast her vote in Rochester, New York. Two weeks later, she was arrested.

At her trial, which made headlines around the country, the judge told the twelve male jurors to find her guilty and did not allow Anthony to speak. He fined her $100.

In 1905, she met President Theodore Roosevelt at the White House to discuss women's right to vote. She was eighty-six years old and died the following year. The Nineteenth Amendment, nicknamed the "Susan B. Anthony Amendment," passed in 1920. Women finally had the right to vote!

Geronimo

Many Native Americans considered Geronimo a hero because he fiercely fought against people settling on their ancestral lands. Yet, his violent tactics made him a villain in the minds of most Americans and Mexicans of his day. Geronimo's real name was Goyahkla, and he was born in 1829 in Arizona or New Mexico. He belonged to the Bedonkohe people, part of the Chiricahua Apache tribe.

By the time he was seventeen, Geronimo had led four raids on the Navajo and Camanche tribes. Tragedy struck when Geronimo was twenty-two. He came home to find his wife, mother, and three small children murdered by Mexican soldiers. The Apache were not at war with the Mexicans at that time.

Finding their bodies changed Geronimo forever. Irrepressible rage boiled up. That devastating day began his lifelong vendetta against the Mexicans.

Geronimo[59]

The Mexicans were not his only problem. The United States had won the Mexican-American War in 1848, gaining most of the Southwest. Now, they wanted all the Indigenous Americans to move to reservations. Yet, the Apache could not bear to live in one place. They were nomads, following the herds of buffalo and other wildlife. Furthermore, the reservation was far from their ancestral lands.

In 1855, Geronimo led 135 Apache warriors, women, and children in an escape from the reservation. They roamed about, raiding American and Mexican settlements. Chased down by five thousand American troops, they eluded capture for five months. Finally, Geronimo surrendered. He spent the next fourteen years in custody at Fort Sill in Oklahoma, where he died.

Henry Ford

Henry Ford was both a hero of industry and a diabolical antisemite. Born in 1863, he only had an eighth-grade education. In 1892, he built a gasoline-powered "horseless carriage" in the shed behind his house. His "quadricycle" had four bicycle wheels and used a two-cylinder, four-horsepower gasoline engine. It wasn't the first car, yet it launched his epic automotive career.

In 1902, Ford opened the Ford Motor Company and began producing the Model A, a two-cylinder, eight-horsepower car. It had a top speed of around sixty-five miles per hour. He also made the "999" race car in 1902. It was the fastest car of its day with a top speed of ninety-one miles per hour.

Henry Ford (r) and his 999 race car with driver Barney Oldfield[60]

Ford's dream was mass-producing a car everyone could afford. In 1908, he introduced the Model T. He paid his workers almost twice what other factories paid. Within a decade, half of all cars in America were the Model T. He produced fifteen million Model T's in factories worldwide.

Ford owned the *Dearborn Independent* newspaper, where he discussed diverse topics. For instance, Ford approved of a minimum wage for workers but did not like labor unions. His most troubling view was blaming the Jews for war, crime, and immorality. Once a week, his paper's front page featured "The International Jew: The World's Problem." Ford felt that the Jews, who he thought controlled the world's banks, were profiting from World War I. He directly encouraged antisemitism in America.

The Wright Brothers

Wilbur (born 1867) and Orville Wright (born 1871) grew up in Ohio, fascinated by machines. Orville built a printing press when he was sixteen. Neither went to college nor finished high school. Instead, they worked together on business ventures like a bicycle shop. Their money from making and selling bicycles funded their dream to invent an airplane.

The winds and hills at Kitty Hawk on North Carolina's Outer Banks were ideal for their experiments. They built a glider in 1900 that could carry a man. Yet, how could they control it? Wilbur spent hours studying birds through binoculars, realizing they changed direction by modifying their wing shape. Using a pulley and cable system, the brothers learned to change their glider's wings like the birds.

However, they needed more lift. They built a wind tunnel in their bicycle shop and experimented. Finally, they hit upon a wing shape with better balance and lift. The next step was an engine. They made their own and also designed a propeller.

First flight at Kitty Hawk. Orville is flying, and Wilbur runs alongside.[61]

December 17, 1903, was the day! Orville went first. Lying on his belly, he flew their "Wright Flyer" about 120 feet in 12 seconds. Wilbur then flew for 59 seconds, covering 852 feet. A local man used their camera to get a shot of the flight. He had never used a camera before, and they weren't sure if he got the shot until they got home and developed the photo. In 1909, they began building and selling airplanes.

Jesse Owens

James Cleveland Owens was born in 1913, the youngest of ten children. When he was nine, his family moved from Alabama to Ohio in the Great Migration. His new teacher asked his name, and he said "J. C."— his family nickname. She wrote it down as Jesse, and it stuck. Jesse's astounding athletic abilities emerged in junior high. He scored a six-foot-high jump and a broad jump of almost twenty-three feet. In high school, he took all the track trophies, even the Ohio state championship, for three years straight.

As a high school senior, Jesse matched or broke three world records. He ran the 100-yard dash in 9.4 seconds, the 220-yard dash in 20.7 seconds, and pulled off a 24-foot,11.75-inch broad jump. College recruiters lined up with offers. However, he chose Ohio State despite it not having a track scholarship. Owens worked his way through college while setting intercollegiate records.

Jesse Owens at the 1935 Berlin Olympics [63]

In only forty-five minutes, Owens broke three world records and tied a fourth at the 1935 Big Ten Championships, despite recently falling down a flight of stairs. Buoyed by his victories, Owens competed in the 1936 Olympics in Germany. Hitler was sure the "superior" Aryan (White) race competitors would trump the other competitors. Owens proved him wrong. He was the first American to win four gold medals in track and field at the Olympics. In the words of President Jimmy Carter, "Perhaps no athlete better symbolized the human struggle against tyranny, poverty, and racial bigotry."

Maya Angelou

Born in 1928 in St. Louis, Missouri, Maya Angelou was an activist, author, dancer, poet, scholar, and singer. She wrote about events in her life, how they changed her, and what she learned from them. Her parents' marriage fell apart when she was three, and her father sent Maya to live with her grandmother. When she was seven, her father abruptly sent her back to her mother, where her mother's boyfriend raped her a year later. The man was murdered, probably by family members, and the trauma caused Maya to be mute for five years. In her silent world, she dove into books and developed a habit of listening, observing, and remembering things.

Maya was sent back to her grandmother, where a teacher, Mrs. Bertha Flowers, helped her to speak again by reciting poetry. Mrs. Flowers introduced her to classic literature and the writings of early Black female activists. At age fourteen, Maya went back to live with her mother. At sixteen, she got pregnant. She was terrified. Decades later, Maya shared about the experience on her Facebook page:

> "Back then, if you had money, there were some girls who got abortions, but I couldn't deal with that idea. Oh, no. No. I knew there was somebody inside me. So, I decided to keep the baby ... I'm telling you that the best decision I ever made was keeping that baby! ... Years later, when I was married, I wanted to have more children, but I couldn't conceive. Isn't it wonderful that I had a child at sixteen? Praise God!"[i]

---

[i] Bre Payton, "Maya Angelou Explains Why She Decided Against An Abortion," *The Federalist*, June 29, 2016, https://thefederalist.com/2016/06/29/maya-angelou-explains-why-she-decided-against-an-abortion/.

Maya Angelou with her first book in 1971[68]

Clyde Bailey (Guy) Johnson was her only child.

Angelou had talent as a calypso and cabaret singer and dancer. In the 1950s, she traveled as a performer around the United States, Europe, and North Africa. She published the story of her childhood and teen years in *I Know Why the Caged Bird Sings*, which became a bestseller. Many other books, plays, and poetry followed. She worked with Martin Luther King Jr. and Malcolm X in the civil rights movement. In Maya's own words, "You may not control all the events that happen to you, but you can decide not to be reduced by them."

Roundup Activity: Essay

Choose a person from this chapter that interests you the most. Write a two-to-three-paragraph essay explaining why this person intrigues you and what lessons can be learned from their life.

Answers to Roundup Questions

Chapter One Roundup Activity Answer Key

Image source[64]

Chapter Two Roundup Activity Answer Key

Most of the colonists in Virginia and New England came from **Protestant** groups. The Lost Colony disappeared from **Carolina's** Outer Banks. Among Jamestown's early leaders, **John Smith** was a former pirate and slave. After leaving England, the Puritans first went to **Holland** before sailing to America. **Squanto**, a Patuxet man, taught the Puritans to farm, hunt, and fish. The Puritans believed all children needed to be **literate**. The Spaniards in Florida offered freedom to slaves who escaped the British colonies and settled them at **Fort Mose**. **Jonathan Edwards** and **George Whitfield** were two ministers who helped spark the Great Awakening.

Chapter Three Roundup Activity Answer Key

(F) 1. The 1763 Treaty of Paris gave the French all the colonies east of the Mississippi River.

(T) 2. The Enlightenment thinkers preferred intellectual reason over faith and tradition.

(F) 3. The British trade policies with the American colonists were fair and profitable for all.

(T) 4. The Boston Tea Party led to the British closing Boston Harbor.

(T) 5. The Green Mountain Boys sent the canons from Fort Ticonderoga to Boston.

(F) 6. The Continental Congress wrote the Declaration of Independence at the war's end.

(T) 7. Thomas Paine's booklet *Common Sense* strengthened the resolve of the Americans.

(T) 8. Washington's troops won the Battle of Trenton on Christmas Day.

(T) 9. The Treaty of Paris recognized American independence and gave Florida back to Spain.

(T) 10. The Bill of Rights included freedom of speech and religion.

Chapter Five Roundup Activity Answer Key

1. Which of the following did Abraham Lincoln believe about Black people?

    d. <u>None of the above</u>

2. Which of the following did Charles Darwin believe about White people?

    d. <u>All of the above</u>

3. Dred Scott lost his court case for freedom because...

    d. <u>All of the above</u>

4. Who got called "Scalawags?"

    c. <u>White people who advocated for formerly enslaved Blacks</u>

5. How did some White people retaliate against the bus boycott by Black people?

    d. <u>All of the above</u>

Chapter Six Roundup Activity Answer Key

Crossword Puzzle: World Wars I and II

Down:
2. not getting involved in other nation's fights
3. staged a surprise attack on Pearl Harbor
4. the side America fought on in WWI
8. where America won a decisive sea battle against Japan
10. where WWI started

Across:
1. American admiral in Pacific during WWII
5. where Nazi Germany's invasion triggered WWII
6. union of Germany, Japan, and Italy against Allies
7. the city where America dropped the first atomic bomb
9. violent dictators with unlimited powers
11. where the Japanese killed 200,000 civilians
12. the war to end all wars
13. America's first WWI battle in France
14. the systematic murder of 6 million Jews

Image sources[65]

Chapter Seven Roundup Activity Answer Key

The underlined statements are untrue.

- The USSR covered one-sixth of the planet at its peak.
- <u>The USSR achieved superpower status before World War I.</u>
- The USSR's political ideology was at odds with American democratic ideals.
- NATO was an alliance of the US, Canada, and European countries to defend themselves against a potential attack from a "third party" (primarily the Soviet Union).
- NATO and the Warsaw Pact alliances set off the Cold War.
- <u>The Cold War ended in 1962 after the Cuban Missile Crisis was resolved.</u>
- <u>Atom bombs are much more powerful than hydrogen bombs.</u>
- The Soviets used captured German nuclear scientists to develop an atom bomb.
- American schoolchildren had drills where they practiced hiding under the desk for protection from nuclear bombs.
- The USSR installed nuclear-armed ballistic missiles in Cuba, only ninety miles from Florida.
- President Kennedy put a navy blockade around Cuba.
- <u>The Soviet missiles never got removed from Cuba.</u>
- <u>America sent the first man-made satellite into space.</u>
- A dog named Laika was the first animal in space.
- America won the Space Race by putting men on the moon.

Chapter Eight Roundup Activity Answer Key

1. How did the first Americans get to America?
    <u>a. They crossed the Beringia land bridge.</u>
2. What did the Indigenous Americans teach the European colonists?
    <u>c. Both a and b</u>
3. Who believed that all children—boys and girls—should be educated?

    b. The Puritans in New England
4. Who wrote the Declaration of Independence?
    d. Thomas Jefferson
5. Which political party was pro-slavery when it first began?
    a. Democrat
6. Whose submarine sank the USS *Housatonic*?
    a. The Confederates
7. Why did Mrs. Rosa Parks get arrested?
    c. Both a and b
8. What was different about World War I?
    d. All of the above
9. Who masterminded the September 11, 2001, attacks on the United States?
    b. Osama bin Laden
10. How did the CIA figure out bin Laden was in the compound in Pakistan?
    d. All of the above

If you enjoyed this book, a review on Amazon would be greatly appreciated because it would mean a lot to hear from you.

To leave a review:
1. Open your camera app.
2. Point your mobile device at the QR code.
3. The review page will appear in your web browser.

Thanks for your support!

Here's another book by Enthralling History that you might like

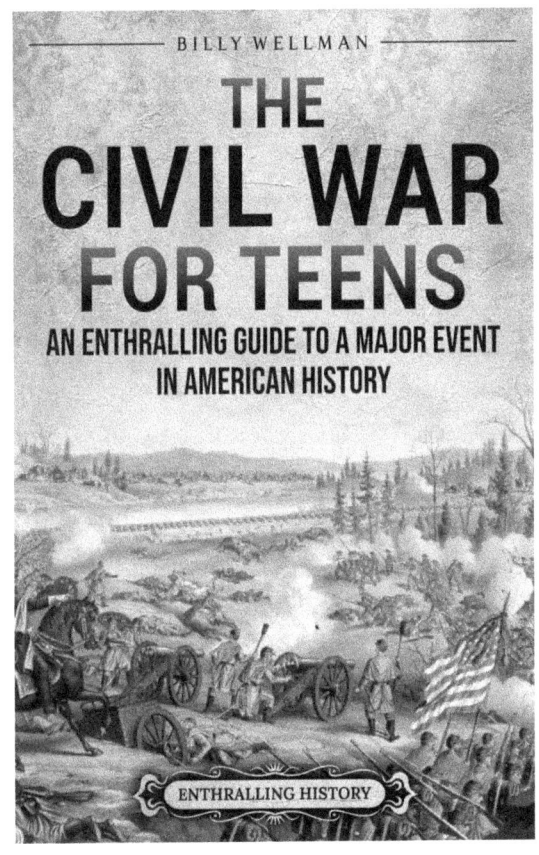

Free limited time bonus

Stop for a moment. We have a free bonus set up for you. The problem is this: we forget 90% of everything that we read after 7 days. Crazy fact, right? Here's the solution: we've created a printable, 1-page pdf summary for this book that you're reading now. All you have to do to get your free pdf summary is to go to the following website: **https://livetolearn.lpages.co/enthrallinghistory/**

Or, Scan the QR code!

Once you do, it will be intuitive. Enjoy, and thank you!

Bibliography

"Americans and the Holocaust." United States Holocaust Memorial Museum. Accessed January 4, 2025. https://exhibitions.ushmm.org/americans-and-the-holocaust/main/state-department-obstruction-1#:~:text=In%20early%201943%2C%20US%20State,from%20reaching%20the%20United%20States.

Barton, David, and Tim Barton. *The American Story: The Beginnings.* WallBuilders Press, 2020.

Bower, Bruce. "American Democracy Arrived Long Before Columbus Did." *Science News Explores: Archaeology,* February 23, 2023. https://www.snexplores.org/article/american-democracy-indigenous-native-people-government#:~:text=The%20peoples%20were%20governed%20through,glue%20holding%20these%20peoples%20together.6.

Bush, George W. "Global War on Terror." George W. Bush Presidential Library. Accessed January 4, 2025. *https://www.georgewbushlibrary.gov/research/topic-guides/global-war-terror.*

Chernow, Ron. *Grant.* Penguin Press, 2017.

Darwin, Charles. *The Descent of Man and Selection in Relation to Sex.*1781. The Project Gutenberg eBook, updated December 27, 2021. https://www.gutenberg.org/cache/epub/2300/pg2300-images.html#link2HCH0005.

Foner, Eric. "Reconstruction." *The Civil War Remembered.* National Park Service. Accessed January 4, 2025. https://www.nps.gov/articles/reconstruction.htm.

Franchi, Rodd. *19th Century American History for Teens: Understanding the Themes, Ideologies, and Conflicts that Inform Our Present.* Rockridge Press, 2021.

Guanghua, Li. "The Influence of Puritanism on the Shaping of Traditional American Values." *International Journal of English Literature and Social Sciences* 6, no. 4 (July-August 2021). https://doi.org/10.22161/ijels.

Keegan, John. *The Second World War.* Penguin Press, 2005.

Kennedy, Randall. "Martin Luther King's Constitution: A Legal History of the Montgomery Bus Boycott." *The Yale Law Journal* 98, no. 6 (April 1989):999-1067. https://www.jstor.org/stable/i232693.

Kidd, Thomas S. *American History, Combined Edition: 1492-Present.* B&H Academic, 2019.

Kidd, Thomas S. *Patrick Henry: First Among Patriots.* Basic Books, 2011.

King, David C. *American History: A Visual Encyclopedia.* Penguin Random House, 2023.

King, Jr., Martin Luther. "'I Have a Dream' Speech." *History,* updated December 19, 2023. https://www.history.com/topics/black-history/i-have-a-dream-speech.

Neely, Mark E. Jr., *The Abraham Lincoln Encyclopedia* (Da Capo Press, Inc., 1982). "Fourth Debate: Charleston, Illinois, September 18, 1858." National Park Service. Accessed January 4, 2025.
https://www.nps.gov/liho/learn/historyculture/debate4.htm.

Nelson, Michael. "'America Is Under Attack': What the Morning of 9/11 Was Like for President Bush." *UVA Today,* September 8, 2022.
https://news.virginia.edu/content/america-under-attack-what-morning-911-was-president-bush.

Paine, Thomas. *Common Sense.* W. & T. Bradford, 1776. The Project Gutenberg eBook. https://www.gutenberg.org/files/147/147-h/147-h.htm.

Payton, Bre. "Maya Angelou Explains Why She Decided Against An Abortion." *The Federalist,* June 29, 2016.
https://thefederalist.com/2016/06/29/maya-angelou-explains-why-she-decided-against-an-abortion/.

Rafe, Jennifer. *Origin: A Genetic History of the Americas.* Twelve, 2022.

"Statement by the President on the Hydrogen Bomb." The American Presidency Project. Accessed January 4, 2025.
https://www.presidency.ucsb.edu/documents/statement-the-president-the-hydrogen-bomb.

Taylor, Alan. *American Revolutions: A Continental History, 1750-1804.* W. W. Norton & Company, 2017.

"The Return of the Spirit: The Second Great Awakening." *Christianity Today.* Accessed January 4, 2025. https://www.christianitytoday.com/1989/07/return-of-spirit-second-great-awakening/.

"WW2 Stories: Five Compelling First-Hand Accounts from D-Day." Warfare History Network. Accessed January 4, 2025. https://warfarehistorynetwork.com/ww2-stories-5-compelling-first-hand-accounts-from-d-day/.

Image Sources

[1] User:Roblespepe, CC BY-SA 3.0 <https://creativecommons.org/licenses/by-sa/3.0>, via Wikimedia Commons: https://commons.wikimedia.org/wiki/File:Peopling_of_America_through_Beringia.png

[2] Garlan Miles, CC BY-SA 4.0 <https://creativecommons.org/licenses/by-sa/4.0>, via Wikimedia Commons: https://commons.wikimedia.org/wiki/File:Three_Sisters_4.jpg

[3] Herb Roe, CC BY-SA 3.0 <https://creativecommons.org/licenses/by-sa/3.0>, via Wikimedia Commons: https://commons.wikimedia.org/wiki/File:Braden_Style_Chunkey_player_St_Marys_Mound_Site_HRoe.jpg

[4] https://commons.wikimedia.org/wiki/File:Columbus_Taking_PossessionFXD.jpg

[5] https://commons.wikimedia.org/wiki/File:De_Soto_by_Telfer_%26_Sartain.jpg

[6] Bwickliffe, CC BY-SA 4.0 <https://creativecommons.org/licenses/by-sa/4.0>, via Wikimedia Commons: https://commons.wikimedia.org/wiki/File:The_Gonzalez-Alvarez_House_Oldest_Surviving_House_in_St_Augustine,_FL.jpg

[7] https://www.education.com/

[8] Photo zoomed in. https://commons.wikimedia.org/wiki/File:The-Lost-Colony_0.jpg

[9] https://commons.wikimedia.org/wiki/File:NPG_65_61_Pocahontas.tif

[10] Internet Archive Book Images, No restrictions, via Wikimedia Commons: https://commons.wikimedia.org/wiki/File:A_popular_history_of_the_United_States_-_from_the_first_discovery_of_the_western_hemisphere_by_the_Northmen,_to_the_end_of_the_first_century_of_the_union_of_the_states;_preceded_by_a_sketch_of_the_(14597125217).jpg

[11] https://commons.wikimedia.org/wiki/File:The_First_Thanksgiving_cph.3g04961.jpg

[12] https://commons.wikimedia.org/wiki/File:Jonathan_Edwards_engraving.jpg#file

[13] AlexiusHoratius, CC BY-SA 3.0 <https://creativecommons.org/licenses/by-sa/3.0>, via Wikimedia Commons: https://commons.wikimedia.org/wiki/File:NorthAmerica1763-A.png

[14] https://commons.wikimedia.org/wiki/File:Joseph_Siffrein_Duplessis_-_Benjamin_Franklin_-_Google_Art_Project.jpg

[15] https://commons.wikimedia.org/wiki/File:Paul_Revere%27s_ride_-_NARA_-_535721.tif

[16] https://commons.wikimedia.org/wiki/File:Washington_Crossing_the_Delaware_by_Emanuel_Leutze,_MMA-NYC,_1851.jpg

[17] https://commons.wikimedia.org/wiki/File:George_Washington_MET_DT220048.jpg

[18] https://commons.wikimedia.org/wiki/File:Frederick_Douglass_(circa_1879).jpg

[19] William Morris, CC BY-SA 4.0 <https://creativecommons.org/licenses/by-sa/4.0>, via Wikimedia Commons: https://commons.wikimedia.org/wiki/File:Louisiana_Purchase.png

[20] Made by User:Golbez, CC BY-SA 3.0 <http://creativecommons.org/licenses/by-sa/3.0/>, via Wikimedia Commons: https://commons.wikimedia.org/wiki/File:United_States_1861-08-1862.png

[21] https://commons.wikimedia.org/wiki/File:Clara_Barton_1865.jpg

[22] https://commons.wikimedia.org/wiki/File:Oil_on_Canvas_Portrait_of_Dred_Scott_(cropped).jpg

[23] https://commons.wikimedia.org/wiki/File:Freedmen%27s_Schoolhouse_Burns_in_1866_Memphis_Riot.jpg

[24] https://commons.wikimedia.org/wiki/File:Ku_Klux_Klan_demonstration_in_Tampa.jpg

[25] https://commons.wikimedia.org/wiki/File:Rosa_Parks_being_fingerprinted_by_Deputy_Sheriff_D.H._Lackey_after_being_arrested_on_February_22,_1956,_during_the_Montgomery_bus_boycott.jpg

[26] David Erickson, CC BY 2.0 <https://creativecommons.org/licenses/by/2.0>, via Wikimedia Commons: https://commons.wikimedia.org/wiki/File:Martin_Luther_King_Jr._-_I_Have_A_Dream_Speech.jpg

[27] Flutellute & User:Bibi Saint-Pol (English translation), CC BY-SA 4.0 <https://creativecommons.org/licenses/by-sa/4.0>, via Wikimedia Commons: https://commons.wikimedia.org/wiki/File:Beginning_of_WWI_in_Europe_(belligerents_in_1914-1915).gif

[28] https://commons.wikimedia.org/wiki/File:Sinking_of_the_Lusitania_London_Illus_News.jpg

[29] Egrim21Egrim21, CC BY-SA 4.0 <https://creativecommons.org/licenses/by-sa/4.0>, via Wikimedia Commons: https://commons.wikimedia.org/wiki/File:Women_Navy_Recruit_Poster.jpg

[30] Michael Kassube, CC BY-SA 3.0 <https://creativecommons.org/licenses/by-sa/3.0>, via Wikimedia Commons: https://commons.wikimedia.org/wiki/File:WWI_postcard_trench.JPG

[31] https://commons.wikimedia.org/wiki/File:USS_SHAW_exploding_Pearl_Harbor_Nara_80-G-16871_2.jpg

[32] https://commons.wikimedia.org/wiki/File:We_Can_Do_It!_NARA_535413_-

_Restoration_2.jpg

[33] SHAEF [Supreme Headquarters Allied Expeditionary Forces] Public Relations Division, Public domain, via Wikimedia Commons: https://commons.wikimedia.org/wiki/File:Normandy_landings_D_Day_to_D_plus_3_Supreme_Allied_Command_footage_(Signal_Corps_catalog_reel_nos_111-ADC-1319,_111-ADC-1318,_111-ADC-2093,_and_111-ADC-1336)_35.png

[34] Photo zoomed in. J Malan Heslop, colorized by Julius Jääskeläinen, CC BY 2.0 <https://creativecommons.org/licenses/by/2.0>, via Wikimedia Commons; https://commons.wikimedia.org/wiki/File:Liberated_prisoner_of_the_Ebensee_concentration_camp_in_Austria,_8_May_1945._(45899003575).jpg

[35] https://commons.wikimedia.org/wiki/File:Nagasakibomb.jpg

[36] https://www.education.com/

[37] Photo zoomed in. https://commons.wikimedia.org/wiki/File:L_to_R_British_Prime_Minister_Winston_Churchill_President_Harry_S._Truman_and_Soviet_leader_Josef_Stalin_in_the..._-_NARA_-_198958_myhritage.jpg

[38] https://commons.wikimedia.org/wiki/File:P.S._58_-_Carroll_%26_Smith_Sts._Bklyn._hold_a_take_cover_drill_01489v.jpg

[39] Photo zoomed in. https://commons.wikimedia.org/wiki/File:LeMay_Cuban_Missile_Crisis.jpg

[40] Mos.ru, CC BY 4.0 <https://creativecommons.org/licenses/by/4.0>, via Wikimedia Commons: https://commons.wikimedia.org/wiki/File:Laika_in_1957.jpg

[41] https://commons.wikimedia.org/wiki/File:Aldrin_Apollo_11.jpg

[42] https://commons.wikimedia.org/wiki/File:National_Park_Service_9-11_Statue_of_Liberty_and_WTC_fire.jpg

[43] https://commons.wikimedia.org/wiki/File:President_George_W._Bush_with_the_National_Security_Council.jpg

[44] Hamid Mir, CC BY-SA 3.0 <https://creativecommons.org/licenses/by-sa/3.0>, via Wikimedia Commons: https://commons.wikimedia.org/wiki/File:Hamid_Mir_interviewing_Osama_bin_Laden_and_Ayman_al-Zawahiri_2001.jpg

[45] https://commons.wikimedia.org/wiki/File:United_States_Armed_Forces_in_the_Gulf_War_1991_GLF1058.jpg

[46] justgrimes, CC BY-SA 2.0 <https://creativecommons.org/licenses/by-sa/2.0>, via Wikimedia Commons: https://commons.wikimedia.org/wiki/File:Bin_laden_death_washington_post.jpg

[47] https://commons.wikimedia.org/wiki/File:Gilbert_Stuart,_George_Washington_(Lansdowne_portrait,_1796).jpg

[48] https://commons.wikimedia.org/wiki/File:Thomas_Jefferson_1805_Portrait_3x4_Crop.jpg

[49] https://commons.wikimedia.org/wiki/File:Abraham_Lincoln_circa_1860.png

[50] https://commons.wikimedia.org/wiki/File:Theodore_Rooseveltnewtry.jpg

[51] Photo zoomed in. https://commons.wikimedia.org/wiki/File:Yalta_summit_1945_with_

Churchill,_Roosevelt,_Stalin.jpg

[52] **Photo zoomed in.:** https://commons.wikimedia.org/wiki/File:President_John_F._Kennedy_with_Robert_F._Kennedy,_Jr._(02).jpg

[53] https://commons.wikimedia.org/wiki/File:President_Ronald_Reagan_and_Prince_Charles.jpg

[54] https://commons.wikimedia.org/wiki/File:Mathew_Brady_-_Franklin_Pierce_(cropped).jpg

[55] https://commons.wikimedia.org/wiki/File:James_Buchanan_(cropped).jpg

[56] https://commons.wikimedia.org/wiki/File:Andrew_johnson2.png

[57] https://commons.wikimedia.org/wiki/File:Benedict_Arnold_1color_(crop).jpg

[58] https://commons.wikimedia.org/wiki/File:Susan_B_Anthony_c1855.png

[59] https://commons.wikimedia.org/wiki/File:Geronimo_(Goyathlay),_a_Chiricahua_Apache,_full-length,_kneeling_with_rifle,_1887_-_NARA_-_530880.jpg

[60] https://commons.wikimedia.org/wiki/File:Henry_Ford_and_Barney_Oldfield_with_Old_999,_1902.jpg

[61] **Photo zoomed in.** https://commons.wikimedia.org/wiki/File:Wright_First_Flight_1903Dec17_(restore_115).tif?page=1

[62] https://commons.wikimedia.org/wiki/File:Jesse_Owens_%C3%A0_Berlin,_JO_de_1936.jpg

[63] https://commons.wikimedia.org/wiki/File:Portrait_photograph_of_Maya_Angelou_with_a_copy_of_I_Know_Why_the_Caged_Bird_Sings_in_Los_Angeles,_November_3,_1971.jpg

[64] https://www.education.com/

[65] https://www.education.com/

www.ingramcontent.com/pod-product-compliance
Lightning Source LLC
Chambersburg PA
CBHW070332010526
44107CB00004B/499